COACHING KIDS SOCCER - AGES 5 TO 10 - VOLUMES 1,2 & 3

BY CHRIS KING

**WANT A FREE SOCCER COACHING eBOOK?
Simply head to
www.chriskingsoccercoach.com
and sign up!**

Or scan the QR code

SOCCER COACHING VIDEO COURSE

If you are a beginner coach I have a great online video course. It includes lots of information, games and tips for childrens soccer coaches.

Email me at **www.chriskingsoccercoach.com** ,

ask for a code and I'll send you a 50%

off discount code! Easy!

To find the course head to this link https://bit.ly/kidscoachingcourse, go to my website chriskingsoccercoach.com or head to **Udemy.com and search "chris king soccer"**.

There is a course for coaching kids and a more advanced course for those coaching youth to adults that want to improve their knowledge and training sessions. Both courses are easy to understand and are aimed at grassroots soccer coaches.

Here's a review from "HOW TO COACH KIDS SOCCER: A COURSE FOR BEGINNER COACHES"

"This Course gives good advice and some really fun games that kids enjoy! The games are skill building without being boring. My U8 soccer team loves them all!" - Paige Twardzik

"Great information and basics to be able to volunteer or step in to be a coach" - Teri Patterson

If you are a soccer coach and have a favourite drill that your kids enjoy, I'd love to hear from you! Say hello and email me a description of the drill to chriskingsoccercoach@gmail.com . I might even include it in one of my future books.

Anyway, let's get into the books so you can become a better grassroots soccer coach!

Let's start with Volume 1....

COACHING KIDS SOCCER - AGES 5 TO 10 - VOLUME 1

BY CHRIS KING

This book is for grassroots soccer coaches, volunteers, parents and any would-be coach.

After reading this, you will be able to plan a 60 minute children's soccer training session, set it up and run it using simple, fun soccer games provided in this book!

This short book will show you how to take a training session that teaches the fundamentals of soccer to children aged between 5 to 10.

It's a great starting point for new coaches, volunteers and parent coaches.

The soccer games in this book are designed to be easy to set up and run, as well as being flexible

to adapt to different numbers of kids and skill levels.

Note: *When coaching kids, I refer to drills as **soccer games**, not **soccer drills**. This is because children want to **play games** a lot more than they want to **do a drill**.*

Don't think too much about being an expert soccer coach - your main job is to encourage and help the children enjoy themselves.

One of my main tips when taking a children's training session is:
NO LAPS, NO LINES AND NO LECTURES.

We want to keep the children playing as much as possible so they are engaged and don't have time to get distracted.

The most effective way to get young children to learn soccer is to just let them play for the majority of the time, be it through a small sided game or fun soccer related games.

This book is designed to be short and to the point so you don't get bogged down and worried about being the best coach in the world.

You can simply pick up this book, use the training session layout that I have designed for you and put any of the soccer games in from this book or any of my other books in the "Coaching Kids Soccer" series (there are currently Volumes 1,2 and 3).

Enjoy!

Chris King

Note:

I have included some blank templates for training sessions and match days for you to fill in and use at the end of this book. Cut your favourite one out and photocopy it to reuse throughout the season!

Before you jump into the book here are some other coaching resources that you may find useful to improve your coaching knowledge.:

WEBSITE: www.chriskingsoccercoach.com

AMAZON:
View my other soccer coaching books on my Amazon Author Page

ONLINE SOCCER COACHING COURSES:
If you are a beginner/intermediate grassroots soccer coach that wants to learn more I have some great online video courses.
They include lots of drills, tips and advice for soccer coaches.
COACHING ADULTS SOCCER COURSE
COACHING KIDS SOCCER COURSE
COACHING WALKING SOCCER COURSE

PODCAST:
For coaching advice and soccer games listen to *"Coaching*

Kids Soccer by Chris King" the podcast. Available on Apple, Spotify and Podbean. Also available on my website.

FACEBOOK www.facebook.com/chriskingsoccercoach

EMAIL: Please feel free to email me at chriskingsoccer@gmail.com

LEAVE A REVIEW:

When you're done reading any of my books, would you please leave an honest book review on Amazon? Reviews are the BEST way to help others, and I check them looking for helpful feedback. Just head to the books page on Amazon. Even if it's just a one line review about what you found helpful.

Other soccer coaching books by Chris King

COACHING CHILDREN SOCCER BOOKS
Coaching Kids Soccer - Volume 1
Coaching Kids Soccer - Volume 2
Coaching Kids Soccer - Volume 3
Coaching Kids Soccer - Volumes 1,2,3
Kicking It With Santa: 20 Fun Christmas Themed Soccer Games

COACHING ADULTS SOCCER BOOKS
Training Sessions For Soccer Coaches Volume 1
Training Sessions For Soccer Coaches Volume 2
Training Sessions For Soccer Coaches Volume 3
Training Sessions For Soccer Coaches Volumes 1,2,3
Attacking and Shooting Drills For Soccer Coaches Volume 1
Attacking and Shooting Drills For Soccer Coaches Volume 2
Soccer Rondos Volume 1
Soccer Rondos Volume 2

COLLECTIONS
The Ultimate Soccer Coaching Bundle Volume 1

110 Drills For Soccer Coaches

----

1 PRE-TRAINING TIPS WHEN COACHING CHILDREN SOCCER

- If possible, arrive early so the activities are set up.

Note: You can lose children's attention very quickly, so by having everything set up as much as possible ahead of time it leads to a smoothly run session.

- When the children start arriving, organise them into a game straight away. This is so they can be getting as many touches on the ball as they can even before training starts! Children come to training to play soccer so let them play as soon as you can! This may mean starting with 1v1 when the first two children arrive and then making it 2v1, 2v2, 3v2 etc as more arrive.

SETTING UP A CHILDREN SOCCER TRAINING SESSION

EQUIPMENT
- 1 BALL PER CHILD
- 15 CONES + 15 FLAT DISCS
- 2 TO 4 MINI SOCCER GOALS (use poles or cones if no goals)
- 4 SETS OF DIFFERENT COLOURED BIBS (5 bibs per set so 20 total)

If you're not sure exactly how many children you will have for the session, it's best to set up a "mirror game" (a copy of the game you have set up next to the other one) just in case you get more than expected.

I like to set the two games up side by side with a channel in the middle where I can stand. This is so I can see both games and keep an eye on everything plus I can distribute balls to both areas.

Use the same coloured cone for one pitch and a different set of coloured cones for the other.

This is so it is clear to the children which pitch is which. (Then, for example, you can say to them "Team 1 and 2 on the pitch with yellow cones, teams 3 and 4 on the pitch with blue cones" and they know where to go straight away).

See the image below for how I set up. This example has 12 children with two 3v3 games.

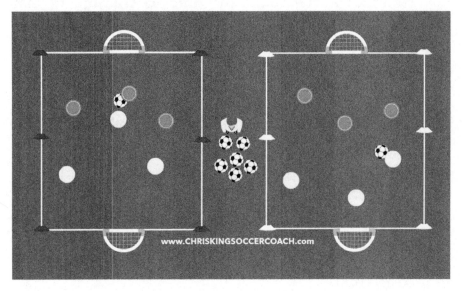

KIDS SOCCER TRAINING SESSION LAYOUT

This is how I run my children's training sessions.

The example below is for a 60 minute session, which allows 50 minutes of training time and a spare 10 minutes for change over of drills, instructions, drink breaks etc.

The session is broken into 5 parts so it is 10 minutes per part (plus the spare 10 minutes).

1. SMALL SIDED GAME - 10 mins

2. FUN SOCCER GAME - 10 mins

3. *SMALL SIDED GAME (*WITH AN EMPHASIS ON THE MAIN SKILL OF THE SESSION) - 10 mins

4. FUN SOCCER GAME - 10 mins

5. SMALL SIDED GAME - 10 mins

KIDS SOCCER TRAINING SESSION PLAN TEMPLATE

That is the session plan layout. Very simple. There are just 5 parts for every training session (and 3 of those are a small sided game).

So you only have to choose 2 Fun Soccer Games to use for each session! How easy is that?

EXAMPLE OF A FILLED IN SOCCER TRAINING SESSION PLAN TEMPLATE (THIS EXAMPLE IS FOR A SESSION ON DRIBBLING)

TRAINING SESSION PLAN   DATE 1.2.23

FOCUS OF SESSION
DRIBBLING

1 **SMALL SIDED GAME**
___4v4___

2 **FUN SOCCER GAME**
___GATES___

3 **SMALL SIDED GAME**
4v4 : REWARD DRIBBLING
ENCOURAGE SKILL BEING WORKED ON
(IE PASSING, DRIBBLING, SHOOTING, 1v1)

4 **FUN SOCCER GAME**
___SIMON SAYS___

5 **SMALL SIDED GAME**
___4v4___

The main thing to take note of with this training session plan is that you should start and finish with a Small Sided Game (Parts 1 and 5).

And Part 3 is simply a Small Sided Game but you make a slight change by **emphasising and rewarding the skill being focussed on that session.**

Only Parts 2 and 4 (Fun Soccer Games) change from session to session.

So in this example, the focus of the session is DRIBBLING.

So I have decided to use two fun games for Parts 2 and 4 that focus on Dribbling. These games are **"Gates"** and **"Simon Says"** which you will find under "FUN SOCCER GAMES" further on in this book.

In a minute, I will show you how to set up the Small Sided Games for Parts 1, 3 and 5 and will give you the Fun Soccer Games to use for Parts 2 and 4.

KIDS SOCCER TRAINING SESSION LAYOUT

Remember this is the order of the session:

1. SMALL SIDED GAME
2. FUN SOCCER GAME
3. SMALL SIDED GAME (with an emphasis on the main skill of the session)
4. FUN SOCCER GAME
5. SMALL SIDED GAME

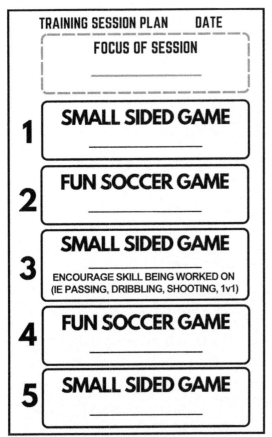

TRAINING SESSION PLAN   DATE

FOCUS OF SESSION

1 SMALL SIDED GAME

2 FUN SOCCER GAME

3 SMALL SIDED GAME
   ENCOURAGE SKILL BEING WORKED ON
   (IE PASSING, DRIBBLING, SHOOTING, 1v1)

4 FUN SOCCER GAME

5 SMALL SIDED GAME

Okay let's get started on showing you how each part works...

SMALL SIDED GAME

(TO BE USED FOR PARTS 1 AND 5)

This is a great way to start the session - simply get the children straight into a game!

They will use up some energy and will get warm. Plus kids come to soccer training to play soccer so why not let them do it straight away?

- Mark out a small field (approx 20x15 metres for a 3v3,4v4 or 5v5 game (adjust the size of the area depending on age and player numbers).

- Organise the children into 2 teams. Try to keep it to 3 or 4 or a maximum 5 per side so that all the players are getting plenty of touches. If there are more than

10 players total, set up another pitch (if you haven't already).

- Tell the kids if a ball goes out, leave it and you'll pass a new one in. This way they get the most amount of game time without having to chase a ball everytime it goes out. If you run out of balls, stop for a minute and get the kids to run and grab them all for you. This saves time and also teaches them to help out.

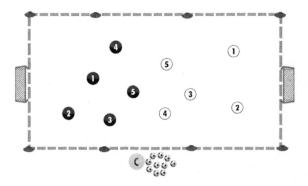

*SMALL SIDED GAME

*WITH AN EMPHASIS ON THE MAIN SKILL OF THE SESSION

(TO BE USED FOR PART 3)

With this part, use the small sided game we just set up. But now add in a slight change to the rules so that you are encouraging the children to work on the main skill of the session.

This part is about introducing a scoring system to encourage certain skills and sportspersonship. But it still stays as a regular, fun small sided game.

For example, if you are teaching the children to dribble, in this game make a goal worth 2 points if they do a good dribble before they (or the team) score.

Here are some examples to implement for Part 3 in your training sessions to encourage different skills etc:

CHANGE 1: A goal is worth 2 points if a different player from the team scores the next goal.

For example, if Martin scores a goal for Team A, can someone different score the next goal for Team A?

What it encourages: *Team play and passing the ball to other players so the same player doesn't hog the ball. Plus kids get their head up to look to pass the ball to a player in a better position.*

CHANGE 2: A goal is worth 2 points if a player beats an opponent before scoring.

For example, if Martin does a turn to get past a defender and scores, his team gets 2 points for that goal.

What it encourages: *Taking on a player 1v1.*

CHANGE 3: A goal is worth 2 points if a player dribbles before scoring or passing to a teammate who scores.

For example, if Martin dribbles out from the back and then passes to Selina who scores a goal, their team gets 2 points.

What it encourages: *Dribbling*

CHANGE 4: A player gets a high five if they shoot at goal (even if they miss).

For example, if Martin usually doesn't shoot but has an attempt and it misses, still give him a high five and say "Great effort!".

What it encourages: *Not being scared to shoot on goal or missing the shot. Encourages them to try different skills without the fear mucking up.*

CHANGE 5: A goal is worth 2 points if there are 3 passes in the lead up to the goal.

What it encourages: *Passing to a teammate.*

CHANGE 6: A goal is worth 2 points if a player scores (or passes in the lead up) with their non-prefered foot.

What it encourages: *Using the weaker foot.*

CHANGE 7: A player gets a high five if they stop a certain goal.

For example, if Martin blocks a shot or kicks the ball away before it crosses the goal line, go and give him a high five!

What it encourages: *Players should defend as well as looking to attack.*

CHANGE 8: A player gets a high five if they help another player up off the ground if they fall over or are tackled and don't get up straight away.

What it encourages: *Good sportspersonship and player bonding.*

Note: Use your imagination and come up with some other ways to reward certain skills or actions that you want your players to focus on. Being a coach means setting a good example as well as being able to think on your feet and change or adjust things when they need it.

FUN SOCCER GAMES
(TO BE USED FOR PARTS 2 & 4)

These fun soccer games listed below are all about children learning a soccer skill while they have fun and enjoy themselves!

With these games, kids will be having a blast while learning the fundamental soccer skills that they need to develop.

Most of the games below can be set up in the areas that you have been using for your small sided games.

FUN SOCCER GAME #1

"GATES"

FOCUS OF THE GAME:
To improve: **DRIBBLING (+ PASSING)**

SET UP:
- 20x20 yard square

- 1 ball each

- Set up 6 'gates' (pairs of the same coloured cones two yards apart) spread randomly around the square.

- Kids will dribble with the ball through the gates as many times in a certain amount of time (1 minute is ideal). Get them to count how many they dribble through and they get one point for each gate.

- *Note*: They cannot dribble back through the same gate until they've been through a different one.

- After each round, ask the children how many gates they got through. Start again and then get them to try to beat that number. This way they are not competing against the best player, they are just looking to improve on their last effort.

PROGRESSION:
#1 -Make the gates wider or smaller depending on the skill level. Also, spread the gates around a bigger area if you want the kids to focus on dribbling and speed. Make the area smaller and gates closer to each other if you want the kids to practise dribbling with lots of traffic around.

#2 - Partner the children up and get them to dribble and then pass the ball through the gate to their partner. This way they can work on passing, teamwork and talking as well as dribbling!

#3 - As the players improve, the coach (or a player) can act as a defender putting light, passive pressure on the players. Players will learn to shield the ball or use speed or a turn to avoid the defender.

COACHES NOTES:

1. Like any skill that someone is learning, focus on doing it correctly instead of quickly. Tell the kids it's not a race, just try their best and try and improve with each round.

2. Tell the children to get their heads up as much as possible. This way they won't run into each other and they can plan which gate is free to dribble through next.

COACHES BONUS TIP:

If you have a very skillful child, put in a couple of really close together cones and then say "If anyone wants to challenge themselves try and dribble through the tight gate". This way they won't think the game is too easy and they can challenge themselves.

Another bonus tip is to hold up a coloured cone in your hand every 15 seconds or so. The player/s that sees the cone and calls out the colour gets a bonus point! This encourages them to get their heads up.

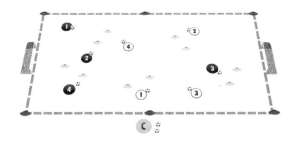

FUN GAME #2
"IT'S A KNOCK OFF"

FOCUS OF THE GAME:
To improve: **SHOOTING (plus DRIBBLING + PASSING)**

SET UP:
- 30x20 yard rectangle

- Split the children into 2 teams and place 3 balls on top of cones at each end.

- Similar to a regular game, but instead of scoring in a goal they aim to knock the opposition's balls off the cones with a pass/shot. The first team to knock all 3 balls off wins!

PROGRESSION:
#1 Make the pitch smaller or larger depending on skill level.

#2 Players can shoot at balls at either end. 1 point for each ball and whichever team has the most points at the end wins.

#3 The coach passes a few balls into the middle at once. This is a bit more chaotic but the kids get to practise more shots!

COACHES NOTES:

1. This drill is all about the children getting used to striking the ball and trying to get a bit of power. They can strike with their laces or a firm pass-shot with their insteps.

2. Tell the children to look at the target but when they are about to strike the ball to look at the ball.

3. Encourage players to still pass the ball if a teammate is in a better position.

COACHES BONUS TIP:

Balls will be going everywhere in this drill! If you have parents standing around that can collect balls, ask them to help out.

Otherwise just go nuts until you run out of balls and then pause the drill and get the children to collect all the balls.

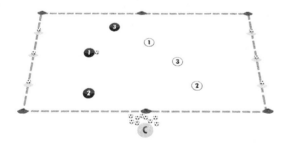

FUN SOCCER GAME #3
"END ZONE"

FOCUS OF THE GAME:
To improve: **DRIBBLING + SHOOTING**

SET UP:
* 30x20 yard rectangle with two end zones 5 yards

from the end.

- 2 mini goals at each end.

- This is similar to the old game of British Bulldog.

- Split the children so there are two defenders without a ball at one end and the rest of the players with a ball at the other.

- Players with the ball dribble and try to get to the opposite end zone and shoot into either goal.

- The 2 defenders try to get a ball off a player and then score at the end the players have just dribbled from. If successful in scoring they swap with the player they took the ball off.

- Once all the attackers have reached the opposite end zone and shot at goal, play restarts in the opposite direction.

PROGRESSION:

#1 Players must use their non preferred foot to dribble or shoot.

#2 Adjust the number of defenders. Is it too easy for the attackers? Add another defender in so there are 3 in the middle. Also you can make it so that the defenders just have to tag the attackers and then they swap roles.

#3 Attackers must perform a skill (a turn/step over/ shoulder drop etc) on their way through the middle.

#4 The coach joins in as a defender! Watch the kids try harder :)

COACHES NOTES:

1. Encourage the attackers to take on the defenders and not be scared. Use this time to practise *changing pace* and a *change of direction* to go past the defenders.

2. Defenders should try and coral an attacker to one side. This way the attacker only has one way to go.

3. Defenders should not over commit to the tackle straight away. Get them to jockey the attacker and then win the ball when the attacker makes a mistake and mis-controls the ball.

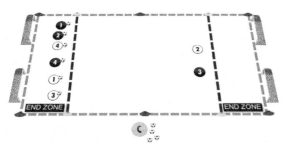

Note on Defending: You don't want your defenders over committing and making it easy for the attackers to get past. They should get out to the player quickly but slow down the last couple of steps and be side on. Then they can jockey the attacker and wait for them to make a mistake before pouncing.

Defenders should:
- Get out quickly to the attacker, then slow down and get low so they can adjust position.
- Bend the knees and have their weight on the balls of their feet.
- When going backwards with the attacker, shuffle their feet (don't cross over feet otherwise they will get

tangled up)

FUN GAME #4
"WORLD CUP"

FOCUS OF THE GAME:
To improve: **DRIBBLING, PASSING, 1v1 + SHOOTING**

SET UP:
- Set up 2 small pitches with mini goals at each end.

- Split the players into teams of two (ie if there are 8 players make 4 teams of 2).

- Teams play each other in 3 minute matches. Teams get 3 points for a win and 1 point for a draw.

- Once all teams have played each other once, total up the points and the top 2 teams play off for the World Cup and bottom 2 play for 3rd place.

- Play is non-stop with the coach passing a new ball into a team as soon as a ball goes out. This keeps the game flowing and makes sure that the children get as many touches on the ball as possible.

PROGRESSION:
#1 If you have an uneven number, the extra player can play as a "joker" and play for both teams by playing for the team in possession. Alternatively put the extra player on the least strongest team.

#2 Have a fun penalty shoot out at the end with the coach as the goalkeeper! But make sure you're having an off day and they score past you more often than not :)

COACHES NOTES:

1. Once again, this is all about having fun! There are no goalkeepers so make sure the kids are shooting and scoring plenty of goals. It's 2v2 so encourage players taking on the defenders and shooting on sight!

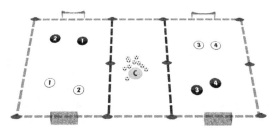

FUN GAME #5
"IT'S A RACE"

FOCUS OF THE GAME:
To improve: **SHOOTING (+ DEFENDING)**

SET UP:
- Set up 2 goals with 4 balls in the middle. Split the children into two teams and number them off.

- The coach calls a number (ie "3!") and the two number 3's race to the middle. The player that gets to the ball first dribbles back and tries to score in the goal from the end they just ran from with the other player trying to stop them.

- First team to 5 points wins.

PROGRESSION:
#1 Call out two player numbers at once so it's 2v2.

#2 Call out two player numbers at once and kick two balls in. 1 point for each goal.

COACHES NOTES:

1. Try and pair similar skill level players against each other if possible.

2. If you don't want to place the balls in the middle, just keep them to the side and kick them in as you call out the number. This way you can kick the ball slightly to the advantage of one player if you want.

3. Make sure the player that doesn't get to the ball first tries their best to defend and stop the goal.

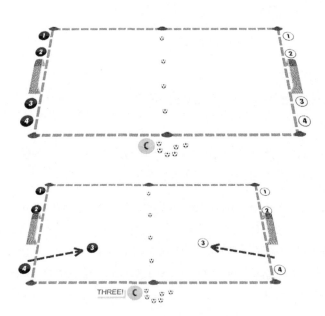

FUN SOCCER GAME #6
"ROB THE NEST"

FOCUS OF THE GAME:
To improve: **DRIBBLING + SHOOTING**

SET UP:
- Set up 4 goals (2 at each end) and a small square in the middle. Place all the soccer balls in the small square.

- Split the players into 4 equal teams with each team starting in one of the corners.

- One player at a time from each group runs out and collects a ball from the centre, dribbles back and shoots at their goal (as soon as they shoot their teammate can start).

- Play until there are no more balls in the centre. The team with the most balls in their goal at the end wins.

PROGRESSION:
#1 Players can steal balls from other teams' goals once all balls from the centre are gone and dribble and shoot it in their goal.

Play for a set time limit and whoever has the most balls in their goal at the end wins.

#2 If you only have enough players for 3 teams, just make a triangle with a goal on each side.

COACHES NOTES:
1. Encourage players to use both feet when dribbling and shooting.

2. Make sure the teammate is concentrating and ready to go as soon as the other player has their shot.

3. The coach can go in the middle and do some passive defending (put some light pressure on players without actually trying to win the ball). As a coach I like to get out in the middle when possible and that way you can encourage and guide players up close instead of calling out from the sideline.

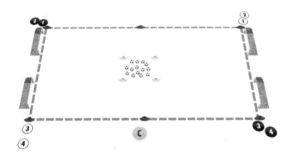

FUN SOCCER GAME #7
"KNOCK IT OFF"

FOCUS OF THE GAME:
To improve: **PASSING**

SET UP:

- Set up 4 cones in the middle of a rectangle with a ball on top of each cone.

- Players pair up with a ball per pair and start 10 yards away at either side of the cone.

- They kick the ball attempting to knock the ball off the cone in the middle in the least amount of passes/kicks possible.

- Take note of how many passes it takes to knock the

ball off (or how many times they knock it off) and then try to beat it on the next attempt.

PROGRESSION:

#1 Depending on skill level, change the distance the players are passing the ball from. Also, I find if they start close and then move back 5 yards each time they hit the ball they improve faster.

#2 If it's too hard, place two cones for the players to pass the ball through instead of knocking a ball off.

#3 Make it a competition between each side or all the pairs: The first side to reach 10 knock off total wins!

COACHES NOTES:

1. Encourage players to use both feet.

2. If you have really young children, work through the passing technique with them slowly. For example, get them to place their striking foot next to the ball, then take a step or two back, then move forward to strike the ball and watch the foot onto the ball.

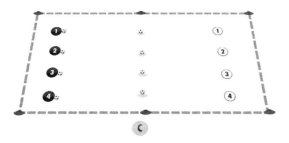

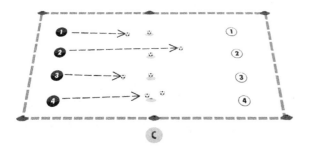

FUN SOCCER GAME #8
"SIMON SAYS"

FOCUS OF THE GAME:
To improve: **DRIBBLING + SKILLS**

SET UP:
- Players dribble a ball inside a marked area.
- The coach calls out instructions for the children to do.
- If the coach says "Simon Says" before the instruction, players do the instruction and then continue to dribble.
- If the coach doesn't say "Simon Says" and a player does the instruction, have them do a small punishment such as 10 toe taps on the ball.
- Examples of some Simon Says instructions are: change direction; stop the ball; stop the ball and put your belly/knee/elbow on it; clap your hands between your legs; skip as you dribble; right foot only; stop your ball and find another; spell their name as they dribble.

PROGRESSION:
#1 If a player gets caught out doing the instruction

when there was no "Simon Says", issue them with a 'Gotcha'. The player/s with the least number of 'Gotcha' at the end win.

#2 If there is a parent or an older player around, get them to give the instructions.

#3 If it's too easy for the players, change the "Simon Says" to simply the players doing the instruction the coach says and then sitting on the ball as soon as they've done it then continue to dribble.

COACHES NOTES:

1. Make this a really fun game. It's a good chance for kids to practise different skills but also to express themselves and have a laugh!

FUN SOCCER GAME #9
"STUCK IN THE MUD"

FOCUS OF THE GAME:
To improve: **DRIBBLING + PASSING**

SET UP:

- All players except two have a ball and are dribbling around the designated area.

- The two players without balls run around and try to

tag the other players. Once tagged, players are *stuck in the mud* and must stop, pick their ball up with their hands and open their legs wide.

- To become unstuck, another player must pass their ball through that player's legs and they are free to dribble again!

- Every one or two minutes change the tagging players.

PROGRESSION:

#1 Have the players dribble with just their left or right foot.

#2 If players are stuck for more than 20 or 30 seconds they become automatically unstuck or every now and then the coach can say "Alakazam!" and everyone becomes unstuck.

#3 If it's too hard or too easy, increase or decrease the amount of taggers.

COACHES NOTES:

1. Make the coach one of the taggers. This way, like I mentioned earlier in the book, you can coach players while you're out there. You can tell them to turn, do a shoulder drop, go and unstick their teammates etc.

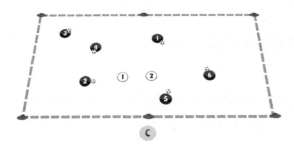

FUN SOCCER GAME #10
"TRAFFIC LIGHTS"

FOCUS OF THE GAME:
To improve: **DRIBBLING**

SET UP:
- Set up two goals at one end and a starting line at the other end where all players line up with a ball. Players attempt to score a goal at the opposite end.

- The coach will call out "Green light!" which signals that the players can run with the ball and "Red light" which signals for players to stop.

- If the coach calls out "Red light" and a player doesn't stop or their ball is too far in front of them, they must return to the starting line.

- If a player scores a goal they get 1 point and return to the starting line.

PROGRESSION:
#1 Call out driving instructions such as "Reverse" (go backwards for 5 yards). Also, instead of calling out instructions, hold up a red or green bib or cone so players must look up to check on the instruction.

Note: This drill can also be done without goals - simply have the players dribbling around in an area and "Green" means go faster, "Red" means stop, "Orange" means turn, etc.

Here are a few tips to keep in mind when training young children.

Please don't gloss over this list.

Read over it a couple of times and keep these ideas front of mind when you are coaching kids.

9 TIPS WHEN COACHING CHILDREN SOCCER

1. You will have players with different levels of skill and experience, so make sure to **encourage and praise all the players** - not just the ones that are at a better skill level.

2. **Be patient** and give them time to grasp what you are showing them.

3. **Praise each child for their effort,** no matter what the end result.

4. Use games that encourage **every child to have a ball at their feet as much as possible.**

5. Create opportunities where **all the children can experience success (ie score a goal, stop a goal, improve a skill).**

6. **Keep the children excited!** Act crazy and be over enthusiastic, the kids will love you.

7. **Use simple language** when you explain something and make sure to demonstrate as well.

8. **Encourage players to be creative.** Soccer should be fun and imaginative - we don't want robots.

9. **Keep it fun** so they will want to come back next time.

SUMMARY

The main focus for most players at this age is to make sure they have fun. If they do, they will keep coming back and will practise and play at home as well. Plus hopefully enjoy playing soccer for the rest of their life.

After the kids finish, I like to try and have a quick word with each one individually as I'm packing up. I mention something that they did really well or have improved on in that session. That way they will go home with a positive feeling.

And remember, you don't have to be an expert coach to coach children. Just give it your best and make sure the kids are enjoying themselves. You'll learn as you go and take more training sessions.

If you enjoy this book, please head to Amazon and spend one minute giving the book a rating to help others find my book.

If you're reading the eBook just go to:

Amazon USA: www.amazon.com/gp/product-review/B09M5HL9KV

Amazon UK: www.amazon.co.uk/gp/product-review/B09M5HL9KV

Or log into Amazon, just head to the products you have bought, click on my book and scroll down to "Write A Review".

Below I've included a few drills from my other coaching books plus some blank training session templates for you to fill in and game day templates.

Feel free to cut your favourite one out and photocopy it to reuse through out the season!

Thanks for your support and happy coaching!

Chris King

Other soccer books by Chris King available on Amazon.
https://amzn.to/3nmgK6B
Follow Chris on Facebook for free drills
www.facebook.com/chriskingsoccercoach
Visit his website to read his blog and see his latest drills
www.chriskingsoccercoach.com

Now available!

DRILLS FROM CHRIS KING'S OTHER "COACHING KIDS SOCCER" VOLUMES

FUN SOCCER GAME "OUCH"

FOCUS OF SESSION:

To encourage the kids to get their heads up while they dribble. This helps them to become aware of where the options are to pass and where the Defenders are.

This drill also helps with striking at a target.

SET UP:

- **5 to 12 players + at least 1 Coach (or parent)!**
- 20x20 yard square

THE DRILL:

What more can a player ask for than to get to kick a ball at the coach? In this game that's exactly what they get to do!

Each player starts inside the square with a ball and the coach starts inside the square without a ball.

When the coach says "Go!" players get to kick the ball at the coach - *aiming for below the knees!* This drill helps with the players being able to strike a ball on the move and also with scanning the area.

Each time the coach gets hit they should yell out "Ouch!" or something silly.

Play for 2 minutes, get the kids to keep count of how many times they have hit the coach and the player that has kicked their ball into the coach the most gets a high five from all the players.

COACHES NOTES:
- Make sure to say that it has to be below the knee for it to count.

- The coach should change directions, dodge and weave so that the players have to look up to see where they are.

- Show the players the correct technique for passing/ striking a ball: Eyes up to look at the target and then eyes back down on the ball to strike it. If it's a close range shot, it can be a pass with the instep. But if it's longer range, show them how to shoot with the laces to get more power.

CHANGE IT:
- If the kids are struggling to hit the coach, slow down and stay in one spot for a second or two to make it easier for them.

- Can players use both feet to dribble and shoot?

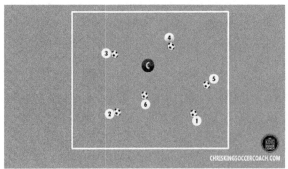

All the players start inside the square with a ball each. Once the coach says "Go!" the coach starts dodging around the square and the players get to pass/strike the ball into the coach (below the knee!).

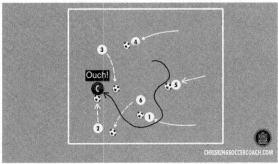

#6 and #3 missed the coach but #2's was a good strike and hit the coach below the knee!

FUN SOCCER GAME
"1v1"

FOCUS OF SESSION:

Good ball control so as to be able to beat an opponent 1v1.

SET UP:

- **6 to 10 players**
- 35x30 yard rectangle
- 6 mini goals

THE DRILL:

Set up a large rectangle (approx 35x30 yards). Place 3 mini goals at each end.

Pair the players up, start at opposite ends with one player with a ball.

The Defender passes the ball to the Attacker who takes control and tries to beat the Defender and score in the goal closest to them at the other end.

If the Defender wins the ball they can try and score in the goal at the opposite end.

Swap roles after each turn.

Note: *Make sure to limit each go to approximately 10-20 seconds. We want to encourage the players to go at the Defender. Not stop, go back, shield the ball, etc.*

COACHES NOTES:

- Make sure the players keep close control. They may want to dribble too fast but they need to keep it under control, otherwise it is easy for the Defender to win the ball. If they have lots of space in front of them they can take longer strides/touches (i.e. have more than 1 step in between each touch). But when the Defender is closer they should be shorter touches (one step for every touch) so they can change direction easily and keep it away from the Defender.

- The Attacker should get their heads up as much as possible so they are away of where the Defender is. They should use different parts of the foot to change direction and get past the Defender.

- Different speeds can also help in getting past opponents. If they send the Defender one way with a feint, can they speed off the other direction?

CHANGE IT:

- Team players up and play 2v2.

- Team all the players up into two teams and play against each other.

- If you don't have enough space or players are getting tired, have 2 pairs behind each other and take it in turns.

- Set up a cone for the players to practise against before moving on to a real 1v1 situation.

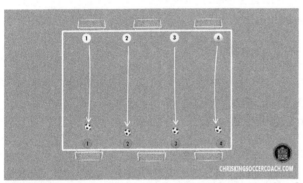

Players get to practise 1v1 situations. Defenders (Yellow) start with the ball and pass the ball to the Attackers to start play.

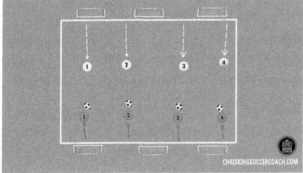

Defenders get out to the Attackers as fast as they can to shut them down. Attackers (Red) get to practise feints, shoulders drops, going at pace, etc to get past their Defender and score in the goal. Swap after each go.

FUN SOCCER GAME
"SURFERS AND SHARKS"

FOCUS OF SESSION:

Dribbling and tackling (and passing when using the progression change).

SET UP:

- **8 to 18 players**
- 35x25 rectangle with 3 different sized small squares inside the area

THE DRILL:

Choose two players to be sharks who wait in the rectangle. The rest of the players are surfers and have a ball and start at one end.

Players practise their dribbling skills, aiming to surf (dribble) from one end of the ocean to the other without getting eaten (tackled) by a shark.

If a shark tackles a surfer and wins the ball they swap roles.

If the surfers need to, they can have a quick rest on one of the islands which are safe zones.

Once surfers reach the other end they turn around and come back. Who can get to the most ends?

<u>Note</u>: *Add or remove sharks if it's too easy or too hard for the surfers.*

COACHES NOTES:

- Encourage players to use different parts of their feet when dribbling (inside and outside of both feet and soles).

- Use a change of speed (or direction!) to get past the sharks.

- Stop the ball on the islands (this will mean that players should have close control so they can stop it when required).

- Shield the ball when required. Can they keep the ball on the other side of the body so the shark can't tackle and steal the ball from them? Players should keep their arms/elbows up to help make them bigger and keep the sharks away from the ball.

- Sharks should look to win possession as soon as they can. If they've just become a shark, encourage them to keep their head up and win a ball back straight away. This helps in a real game situation as they won't give up if they lose a ball they will get in the habit to try and win back possession for their team straight away.

- Make sure surfers aren't spending too long on the islands. If they do bring in a 5-10 second limit.

CHANGE IT:

#1 - Add players to the side and the surfers can do a one two pass with them to avoid being caught with the ball.

#2 - Add goals at each end. If surfers successfully make it from one end to the other they can have a shot at goal and receive a bonus point. Play for 5 minutes and see who gets the most points.

#3 - Team players up and see if they can pass their way

through the ocean without being eaten by the sharks!

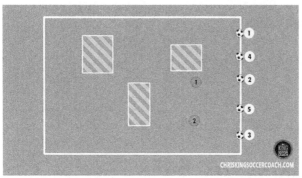

The two red sharks wait in the middle to see if they can catch a surfer and win the ball off them!

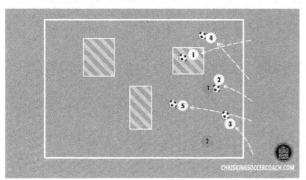

Yellow #4 is smart and goes wide away from the sharks. Yellow #1 goes straight for the first island and is safe and can plan their next move. Yellow #2 get eaten by a shark and must swap roles and become the shark.

TIPS FROM CHRIS KING'S "50 TIPS ON HOW TO COACH A KIDS SOCCER TEAM"

50 TIPS ON HOW TO COACH A CHILDREN'S SOCCER TEAM -AGES 3 TO 6-
Soccer drills, training session tips, game day advice, how to be a good coach, plus much more!

This short book is aimed at taking you - the beginner coach, volunteer or parent - from never having coached a soccer team before, to feeling confident and having fun while coaching a children's soccer team of 3 to 6 year olds.

It has lots of tips that will save you time and give you confidence plus 8 easy to set up kids games that you can use at training.

This book covers topics such as:
- how to set up and run a training session
- how to prepare for match day
- games to use at training
- how to be a good coach
- how to deal with different types of players

- plus many more tips and advice

This book is meant to be short, easy to read and give you so valuable tips to start coaching kids! It's not a huge book where you may get overwhelmed - it has 50 tips that will give you a great head start when coaching kids soccer. So pick up this book and take the first steps to becoming a kids soccer coach!

Chris King

TIP 14 - WHAT TO TEACH KIDS AT TRAINING: SOCCER SKILLS. Most children at this age will not have played soccer before or perhaps it's only their second season.

So you just want to introduce them to the basics of soccer which are: ***Dribbling; Passing; Shooting; 1v1.***

If you can focus on one or two of these main skills the kids will improve week by week.

Note: At this age focus on individual skills, not team tactics.

TIP 15 - WHAT TO TEACH KIDS AT TRAINING: SOCIAL SKILLS. Teaching the kids how to pass, dribble etc is important in soccer. But so is teaching them values such as working as a team, cooperating, taking turns and how to be a good winner and loser. If you do your job correctly, you will be setting them on a path of being a good person for the rest of their lives.

Side note: Make sure they are interacting socially with the other kids. Mix up the players when they partner up so they aren't always with their best friend.

TIP 17 - **NO LAPS, LINES OR LECTURES AT TRAINING!**
Repeat again: No laps, lines or lectures! Thou shalt not make your players do laps. Thou shalt not use drills that involve your players waiting in long lines. Thou shalt not lecture thy players.

Keep these three things in mind and it will go a long way to making sure the children enjoy training!

Why is this? The first two (no laps or lines) are because we want the maximum amount of time and touches on the soccer ball at a training session! If players are doing laps or waiting in line they aren't getting touches on the ball. They've come to soccer training to play soccer, so don't make them do laps of the ground or stand in lines waiting to have one kick of the ball every 2 minutes.

Imagine how many extra touches of a soccer ball children will have over a season if your drills *don't* involve waiting in lines or running laps without touching a ball?

"No lectures" refers to the coach spending too much time talking about what they will be doing that session and explaining drills. Children (and teenagers and adults!) usually only listen to the first few instructions and then they tune out anyway or can't remember all of them.

So don't waste time talking for five minutes when one minute would have been enough and the kids could've been playing for the other four minutes. They come to soccer training to play and run around - save the lectures for the classroom.

TIP 36 - **SHADOW AN EXPERIENCED COACH.**
If you are new to coaching and want to get some

experience, a great way to start is to 'shadow' another coach. Simply ask someone at the club if there is another kids coach that you can follow round for a training session or two to learn off. This way you can see how they set up drills, how they interact with the children, where things are kept at the club, etc.

After you've shadowed the coach for a session or two, you can ask them if you can run one of the drills at the next session. This way there isn't as much pressure as taking a whole training session and you have the other coach there to help you out if you get stuck!

TRAINING & MATCH DAY TEMPLATES

TRAINING TEMPLATE

Use the following 3 page template to plan your soccer training session. Cut them out and photocopy them all onto one A4 page for ease of use. Then fill it in as follows:

1. Fill in the 'Focus Of The Session". For example: *Dribbling*

2. If you know how many players you will have at your training session, fill in the amount of players for the Small Sided Game in Parts 1,3 and 5 (also adding the skill being worked on into Part 3 - which in this example is *Dribbling*). For example if you have 8 players it will be 4v4.

3. Fill in the name of the games you will use for the Fun Soccer Games in Parts 2 and 4.

For example: *Gates* and *Simon Says.*

4. When you've completed the above steps, if you have 8 players at your training session and you

want to focus on dribbling, it should like this:

5. Now you can fill in the two pages of the Fun Soccer Game for Parts 2 and 4. Drawing the drill in the blank rectangle and writing in the Set Up, Description, Progression and Coaches Notes in the other two blank rectangles. This will become quicker and more succinct as you have more experience and training sessions under your belt - it should only take 5 or 10 minutes.

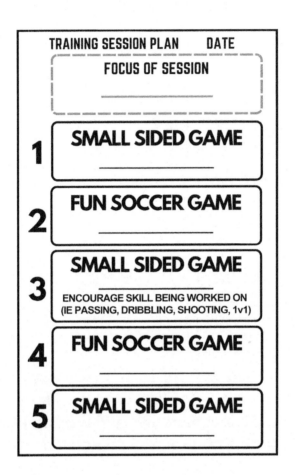

FUN SOCCER GAME 1 : _____

SET UP:

PROGRESSION:

COACHES NOTES:

FUN SOCCER GAME 2 : _____

SET UP:

PROGRESSION:

COACHES NOTES:

MATCH DAY TEMPLATES

Use the following templates for your match day teams and line ups, using whichever ones work best for you. Remember to cut it out and photocopy it to use for the whole season if you want to.

Thanks again! And if you've got some useful information from this book, please head to Amazon and spend one minute giving the book a rating as it helps other coaches find my books.

If you're reading the eBook just go to:

Amazon USA: www.amazon.com/gp/product-review/B09M5HL9KV

Amazon UK: www.amazon.co.uk/gp/product-review/B09M5HL9KV

Many thanks and happy coaching!

Chris King

_____ v _____   **DATE** _____

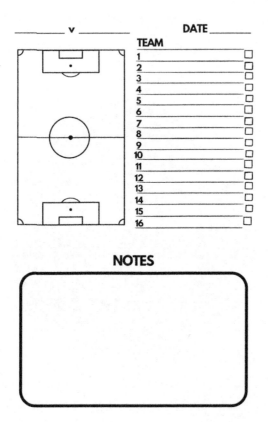

TEAM
1 _____ ☐
2 _____ ☐
3 _____ ☐
4 _____ ☐
5 _____ ☐
6 _____ ☐
7 _____ ☐
8 _____ ☐
9 _____ ☐
10 _____ ☐
11 _____ ☐
12 _____ ☐
13 _____ ☐
14 _____ ☐
15 _____ ☐
16 _____ ☐

NOTES

_____ v _____   DATE _____

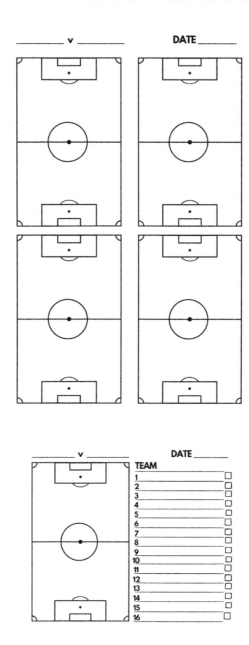

_____ v _____   DATE _____

TEAM

1
2
3
4
5
6
7
8
9
10
11
12
13
14
15
16

CHRISKING

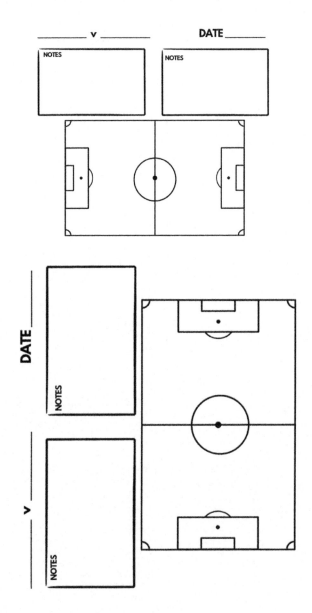

66

COACHING KIDS SOCCER
- VOLUME 2 -
BY CHRIS KING

This book is for coaches, volunteers, parents and anyone that wants to learn about coaching soccer.

I've done all the work for you! I've put together all the skills and games that you will need. In this book you will learn how to teach kids the essential skills they will need plus you will be able to set up simple, fun and effective games and drills.

So if you're ready to learn soccer games such as "Space Invaders", "Zombies" and "Shipwrecked With Sharks" let's get started!

———————————————————————————

Hello coaches and soccer fans!
Welcome to Volume 2 of Coaching Kids Soccer.

I had plenty of interest in the first volume so I decided there's definitely a need to continue to help with the coaching of our future soccer stars!

This book will be structured the same as the first one but it will be a lot longer. **I have included the key skills that**

kids need to learn early on to build a solid foundation for (hopefully) playing soccer their whole lives.

This book is intended for people who are coaching kids (approximately aged between 5 and 10) the basics of soccer.

It's a great starting point for coaches as the drills are designed to be easy to set up and run, as well as being **flexible to adapt to different numbers of kids and skill levels.**

Don't think too much about being an expert coach - your main job is to encourage and help the children enjoy themselves. **All the drills in this book will show you how to run a fun practice session.**

The most effective way to get young children to learn soccer is to let them play via games and fun drills.

This book **includes instructions and images** of how to run practice sessions and **includes different drills and games** for each of the main parts of a practice session.

Enjoy!

Chris King

WEBSITE: Head over to www.chriskingsoccercoach.com to sign up for a free eBook of soccer drills!

AMAZON: View Chris' other soccer coaching books on his Amazon Author Page: www.amazon.com/author/

chriskingsoccercoach (and if you've got a minute, leave a book review while you're there please).

FACEBOOK: Join other like minded coaches and players on Chris' Facebook page: www.facebook.com/ chriskingsoccercoach .

TIPS ON HOW TO COACH KIDS

Before getting into the training sessions, here are a few things to keep in mind when coaching young children:

- You will have different levels of skill and experience amongst the children so make sure to **encourage and praise all the players** - not just the ones that are at a better skill level
- Create opportunities where **all the children can experience success**
- **Be patient** and give them time to grasp what you are showing them
- Use games that encourage **every child to have a ball at their feet as much as possible**
- **Praise each child for** *their effort* no matter what the end result
- **Keep the children excited!** Act crazy or be over enthusiastic if you need to
- **Use simple language** to explain and make sure to demonstrate as well
- **Encourage players to be creative**
- **Keep it fun** so they will want to come back next time

PRE-PRACTICE TIPS

- If possible, arrive early so the activities are set up - it will save you time during the session and it will run smoother
- When the children start arriving, organise them into a game straight away (if there are 3 or 4 kids there get them into a 2v2 game! They're here to play so get them straight into it. A couple of parents can always join in at the start to make up numbers)

EQUIPMENT NEEDED FOR A COACHING SESSION
- 1 ball per child
- Approx 12 cones
- 2 or 4 mini goals (use poles or cones if no goals)
- 4 sets of different coloured bibs

(Note: You can pick up cones, bibs, balls and small fold out goals fairly cheap these days. So if you can, it would be worth spending a small amount of money - or asking the club - at the start of the season so you can keep all the gear together and have it ready to go at each session)

SETTING UP
If you're not sure exactly how many children you will have for the training session, it's best to **set up an extra "mirror drill"** (two of the same drill) just in case.

I like to set the two areas up side by side with a channel in the middle where I can stand and see both areas. Therefore keeping an eye on everything plus I can distribute balls to both areas. (You can lose children's attention very quickly, so by **having everything set up ahead of time as much as possible, it leads to a smoothly run session**).

Use the same coloured cone for one pitch and a different set of coloured cones for the other so it is clear to the children which pitch is which. (Then, for example, you can say to them "Team 1 and 2 on the pitch with blue cones" and they know where to go straight away).

See the images below for how I set up (this example has 12 children with two 3v3 games with the coach in the middle with the balls).

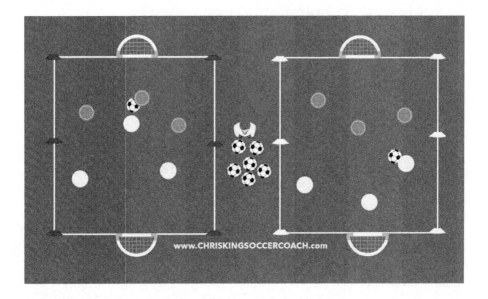

OK, that's some general tips on coaching kids and how I like to set up a training session. Here's how the rest of the book will look:

This book is divided into three parts:

PART 1: TRAINING SESSION: FUN SOCCER GAMES

In *"Part 1: Training Session: Fun Soccer Games"*, you will be shown how to run a training session using fun games that incorporate all the skills your players are learning.

PART 2: ESSENTIAL SOCCER SKILLS

In *"Part 2: Essential Soccer Skills"*, we will run through some key skills to start with.

1. GETTING USED TO THE BALL: Toe Taps; Sole Rolls

2. TURNS: Drag Back; L-Turn

3. DRIBBLING: How To Dribble; Inside Out

4. BEAT A PLAYER: Shoulder Drop + Inside Chop; Double Step Over

PART 3: FURTHER SOCCER SKILLS

In *"Part 3: Further Soccer Skills"* there are more slightly advanced skills the players can progress to which add to their essential skills.

1. BALL CONTROL: Happy Feet; Inside & Outside of Feet; Triangles; Squares; Pull-Push Patterns

2. PASSING: Basic Inside of the Foot Passing; Striking the Ball with the Laces; Basic Receiving Skills

3. JUGGLING: Juggling Basics; Foot Surfaces Juggling Challenge; Heights Juggling Challenge

In Parts 2 and 3 you will be shown skills that kids need to learn when they are first getting into soccer.

In this part (Part 1) you will learn how to structure a training session plus you will be provided with skill based games to use.

This next bit was covered in my first book "Coaching Kids Soccer - Volume 1 - Ages 5 to 10" but it is the best way to structure a training session for children so I have included it in this volume as well.

So read on as I make your life easier as a soccer coach...

HOW TO STRUCTURE YOUR TRAINING SESSION

I would encourage you to structure your training session the same as I have laid out below. Children like a bit of structure. So if you follow the session layout you will find that children soon get to know what to do as the season progresses which makes life easier and more enjoyable.

(**Note:** If you coach youth/adult teams as well, my book "Training Sessions For Soccer Coaches Book 1" lays out how to structure training sessions for youth and adult teams plus all the drills to use).

My training sessions are broken into 5 Parts. If you are running a 60 minute session, I recommend 10 minutes for each part.

Note: This allows 5 to 10 minutes spare for showing and explaining drills. I break each training session down into 5 Parts (not including "Pre-Training: Small Sided Game" which is simply getting the kids playing as soon as they turn up)

PRE-TRAINING: SMALL SIDED GAME - As children arrive up until official training start time

PART 1: ESSENTIAL SKILL PRACTICE - 10 minutes

PART 2: FUN GAME - 10 minutes

PART 3: SMALL SIDED GAME (with a slight change) - 10 minutes

PART 4: FUN GAME - 10 minutes

PART 5: SMALL SIDED GAME - 10 minutes

PRE TRAINING: SMALL SIDED GAME	PART 1: ESSENTIAL SKILL PRACTISE	PART 2: FUN GAME	PART 3: SMALL SIDED GAME (with slight change)	PART 4: FUN GAME	PART 5: SMALL SIDED GAME
Kids go straight into a game as they start arriving at training.	Practise a skill that will be the focus of the session. (ie Passing; Dribbling; 1v1; Shooting)	Fun games related to soccer. A chance for kids to spend time on the ball & experience success.	3v3 up to 5v5 on a small pitch with goals. Encourage the main skill that is the focus of the session.	Fun games related to soccer. A chance for kids to spend time on the ball & experience success.	3v3 up to 5v5 on a small pitch with goals.

One of the main points with this training session structure is that you should have a Small Sided Game (Part 3 and Part 5). This allows the children to learn by doing. They can put the skills and knowledge they have been learning into practise. Children learn by doing, so we want a balance of isolated skill practise and "open" play where they can discover the game of soccer and learn what they are capable of.

I will show you how to set up the small sided games in Part 3 and Part 5 and will give you variations of both Part 2 and 5 (Fun Games) plus the variations for Part 3 (Small Sided Game with a Slight Change).

Remember this is the order of the session:

KIDS TRAINING SESSION STRUCTURE
0. PRE-TRAINING: SMALL SIDED GAME (AS CHILDREN

ARRIVE)
1. ESSENTIAL SKILL PRACTICE
2. FUN GAME
3. SMALL SIDED GAME (WITH A SLIGHT CHANGE)
4. FUN GAME
5. SMALL SIDED GAME

Okay let's get started on the first section...

PRE-TRAINING: SMALL SIDED GAME

This is a great way to start the session before it's actually started! As kids turn up - simply get the children straight into a game! It might be a 10 minute gap between the first child arriving and the last so as a couple have turned up, give them a bib and let them loose in a game! Parents can join in to make up the numbers to start with.

1. Have a small field marked out (approx 20 x 15 metres)

2. Organise the children into 2 teams as they turn up and distribute bibs (try to keep it to a maximum of 4 or 5 a side so that all the players are getting plenty of touches. If there are more than 8-10 players, get another game going in the next square)

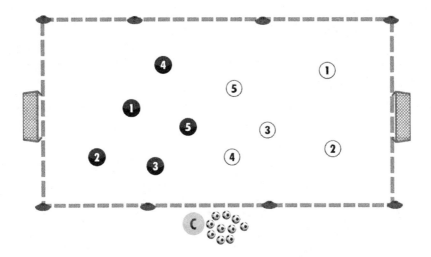

PART 1: ESSENTIAL SKILL PRACTICE

This is the time where we want the children to get lots of touches on the ball and work on their essential/fundamental skills.

Get them all to grab a ball and then show and tell them what skill they will be working on in this training session.

If it's with really young players, it may just be showing them how to do Toe Taps or Sol Rolls. If this is the case, show and tell them how to do it and get them straight into it (they learn by doing)! Then you can go around as they practise and help them out individually.

Stop them after a minute or two and re-show them and get one of the kids to show everyone the skill as well.

If they are older players you may be working on Turns or Passing. If this is the case, in the following Parts (Part 2 through to Part 5) try to make sure to emphasise and encourage Turns or Passing as they play.

PART 2: FUN GAME

This is a game related to soccer and is the chance to get all the children to experience success.

It should focus on a core skill such as dribbling, passing, control, 1v1 or shooting.

Here are 5 different games to use for Part 2 of your training sessions:

FUN GAME #1
"FIRST TO THE BALL"

1. Set up a pitch with a goal at each end and balls positioned on the halfway line (**note**: *see "TIP" at the end of the description for a non-goal scoring, play anywhere version of this drill!*).

2. Split the players into pairs, give one player from each pair a bib and number them off (i.e. if there are 4 players on each team number them off 1,2,3,4) with one from each pair starting at each end along the goal line.

3. The coach calls out a number (ie "Number 3!") and the two Number 3 players race out and battle for the ball.

4. The player that gets to the ball first turns around and tries to score in the goal from the side they came from while the other player tries to stop them.

5. 1 point for each goal and the first team to 5 points wins!

Note: Limit each go to approximately 30 seconds (call it a draw if they haven't scored by then) so the other players aren't waiting around too long.

PROGRESSION:
#1. Call out two numbers and players from the same end join forces to score or defend!

#2. Call out a number from one side and a different one from the other side so players battle against a different opponent.

WHAT TO FOCUS ON:
- Dribbling and taking a player on
- Awareness and quick reactions
- If the player is second to the ball try and get goal side (defensive side) quickly to make it hard for the other player
- Finishing under pressure
- Sportsmanship (get players to say "Well done" if the opponent was too good)

TIP:
If you don't have any goals you can get the kids to be the first to bring the ball back to you instead of shooting at goal. *So this drill is a good one to have in your back pocket as you can do it anywhere.* Just quickly number players off in pairs and then you can kick the ball and call out two numbers!

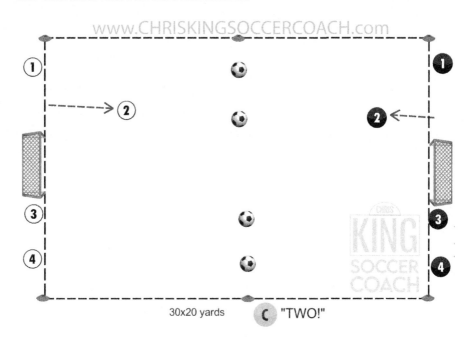

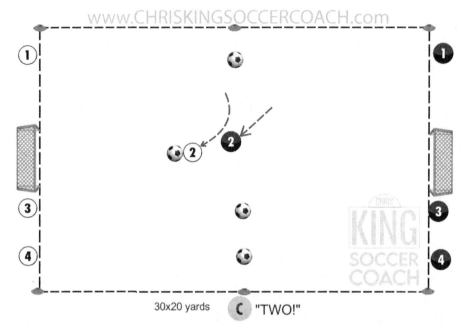

30x20 yards "TWO!"

Summary of "First To The Ball" :

- The Coach calls out "Two!". The player from each end that was given the number 2 runs out and tries to get to the ball.

- In this case the White 2 gets there first so they turn back and try to score in the goal they came from while the Black 2 tries to defend.

- Play until either: the goal is scored; Black 2 wins the ball; or 30 seconds are up.

FUN GAME #2
"BARCELONA"

1. This game is all about passing and scoring but with a twist! It's very easy to set up and will help the kids with maths at the same time as having fun!

2. Set up a small field (20x30 yards) with small goals at each end.

3. Split the players into two teams (3v3 up to 5v5 works best) with no goalkeepers.

4. Regular soccer rules.

5. When a team has possession, count up the number of passes they make and if a goal is scored at the end, that team gets that amount of goals (ie if the team passes 8 times and scores they get 8 points! If they pass 3 times and score they get 3 points).

6. First team to 20 points wins.

7. <u>Note</u>: If the ball goes out take kick ins or the coach passes a new ball in.

WHAT TO FOCUS ON:
- Short passing and moving
- Good close ball control
- Move into space (can a player not on the ball lose their defender by doing a little shoulder drop and going in the other direction?)
- Work as a team

CHANGE IT:
Play 3 rounds of 2 minutes each and add up the total at the end instead of it being the first team to 20 points.

TIP:
Let the players play and you just observe. Save the feedback until the end of a round.

PROGRESSION:
Every player must touch the ball before a goal can be scored. This helps keep everyone involved plus you will see the talk improve and heads look around as the team communicates to make sure everyone has had a touch.

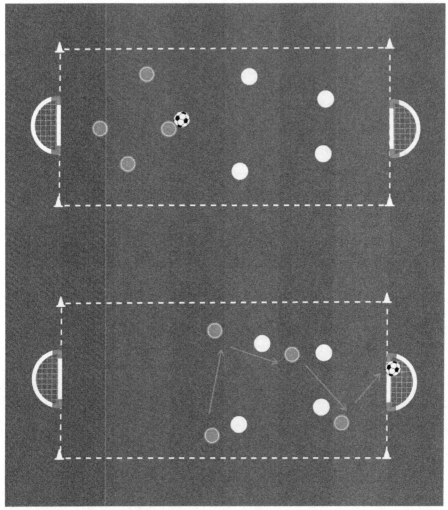

Summary of "Barcelona" :

- Regular soccer but with a scoring twist.

- Each team passes until they score a goal. But make sure to count up the number of passes before the goal because the team gets this amount of points for the goal! (ie if they had 5 passes before scoring they get 5 points!).

- First team to 20 points wins.

- In the above image the Dark team have made 3 passes and then scored so they receive 3 points.

FUN GAME #3
"SHIPWRECKED WITH SHARKS"

1. In this game players are shipwrecked on an island and have to get to another island without the sharks in the middle getting them.

2. Set up a square field (30x30 yards) with small squares marked out in each of the corners (these are the safe "islands").

3. Pick 2 players to be sharks and the rest start on the islands with a ball each.

4. When the coach says 'Go!" players try to dribble from island to island without getting eaten (tagged) by a shark!

5. If the player gets tagged they leave their ball and become a shark.

6. Get the players to count how many islands they get to and see who got the most when the last player gets eaten. Then pick new sharks and start again!

WHAT TO FOCUS ON:
- Scan the area and look for good opportunities to get to the other islands
- Use quick burst of speed
- Quick changes of directions to throw off the sharks
- Encourage players to leave the island and take risks

- Keep their heads up when they are out in the water so they can see where the sharks are

CHANGE IT:

#1. Make the islands bigger or smaller depending on skill level.

#2. Only have one shark if you don't have many players. Or have the coach as the shark (consider going after the stronger players first - this will give the more shy players a chance to get into the drill and gain confidence)!

PROGRESSION:

#1. Instead of tagging a player, the sharks have to win the ball or knock it away and outside the square for the other players to become sharks.

#2. Instead of players joining the other two sharks in the middle, if a player gets eaten/tagged, they have to do 10 toe taps and then they can rejoin the game. Go for two minutes and then swap sharks.

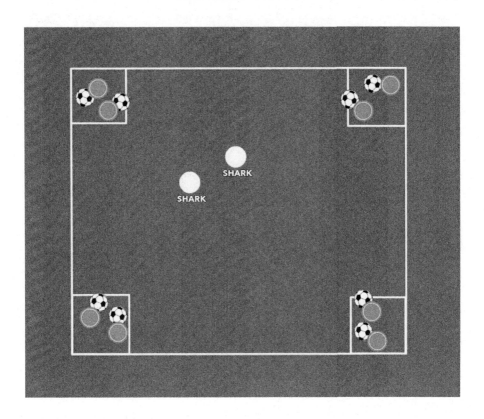

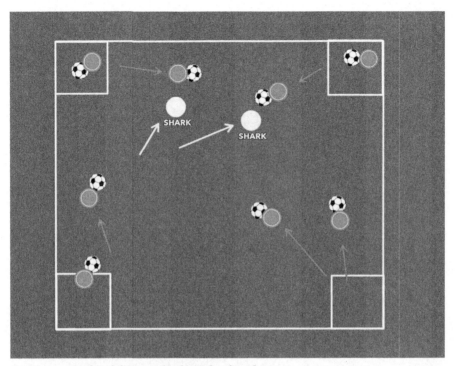

Summary of "Shipwrecked with Sharks" :

- Players start on a safe island and must dribble to the next island without getting eaten (tagged) by one of the sharks that are out in the ocean.

- If a player gets tagged they become a Shark as well and patrol the water looking for a shipwrecked victim to tag.

- Which player can get to the most islands by the end of the round?

FUN GAME #4
"ZOMBIES"□

This is a fun drill that gives the players a chance to work on their dribbling skills and turns. And it gives the parents/coaches a chance to act like a zombie!

1. Set up a square field (30x30 yards).

2. Ask any parents/coaches standing around to join in. They will be the "obstacles" for the children to avoid and will be walking around the square with their arms outstretched like a zombie, saying zombie things like "Braiiinsss" "Graaaghhh" "Childreeenn" "Bananaaaa" and other stupid things or just general grunting noises.

3. Each player has a ball and must dribble around the square avoiding the zombies.

4. If a player gets too close, zombies should lightly kick their ball so they will learn to keep closer control. Or slightly push/bump the player to test their control and balance under pressure.

5. Make sure players are looking around as they dribble and practice turns and changes of direction.

WHAT TO FOCUS ON:
- Players keep close ball control so zombies can't get the ball.
- Use changes of direction to avoid the zombies.
- Keep their heads up when they can to avoid other players and zombies.

CHANGE IT:
#1. Make the area bigger or smaller depending on skill level/ number of players plus the number of zombies.

#2. Make the zombies walk faster or slower depending on the level of players.

#3. If a player gets touched by a zombie they have to do 5 toe-taps and then they can continue dribbling.

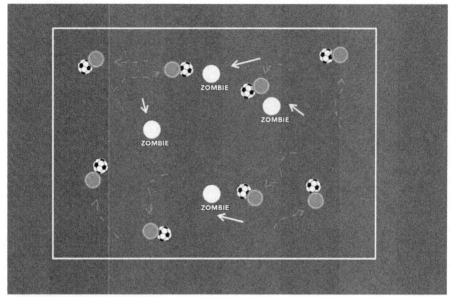

Summary of "Zombies" :

- Players must dribble around in a marked area and try not to get their ball kicked by one of the Zombies walking around!

- Players should be **using turns and keeping the ball on the outside of their body** away from the Zombies

- In the above image, the 4 light coloured Zombies are walking around slowly providing a moving obstacle for the kids to dribble around or practice doing a turn to get away

FUN GAME #5
"SPACE INVADERS"

This game is great for passing, dribbling, evading and close control. Basically everything players should be working on at this stage of their development!

1. In pairs with one ball per pair, players line up on either side of a 10 yard wide channel - these players are the Space Invaders and their balls are their lazers.

2. 2 or 3 players start at one end in the safety zone of the channel with a ball each. These are the Rocket Ships that the Space Invaders are trying to shoot down.

3. The aim of the Rocket Ships is to dribble to the other end of the channel **without getting their ball hit** by a "Space Invader" on the outside.

4. If a Rocket Ships ball is hit by a Space Invaders ball they swap roles.

5. Count up how many times a Rocket Ship can get to each end and see if the player can beat their best on their next run.

WHAT TO FOCUS ON:
- Rocket Ship players dribbling quickly but keeping close control and looking around.
- Space Invaders passing accurately with pace.

CHANGE IT:
Keep the Rocket Ships in for a set amount of time (i.e. 1 minute) and count up how many times a pair of Space Invaders hit the Rocket Ships balls. Then swap at the end of the minute and see who was the best pair of Space Invaders.

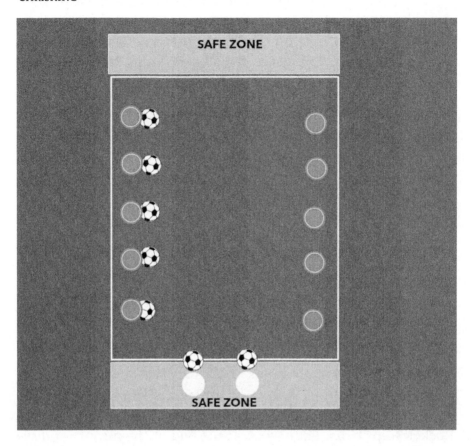

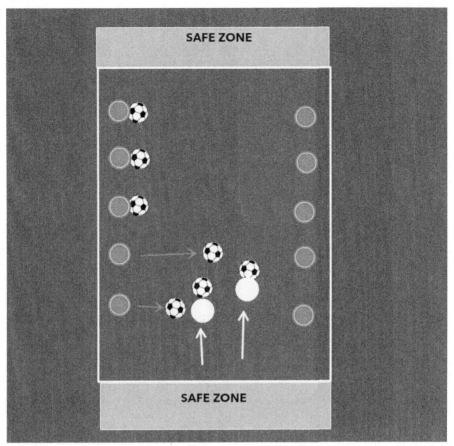

Summary of "Space Invaders" :

- Space Invaders line up in pairs along the side with a ball.

- Rocket Ships (light coloured players) try to dribble through the middle from one end to the other without getting their balls hit by the ball (lazers!) of the Space Invaders who are passing to each other.

- If a Rocket Ship gets their ball hit by a Space Invaders ball they swap places.

- In the above image, once the two light coloured Rocket Ships have started dribbling into the area, the Space Invaders (Dark) can start passing their balls across the area trying to hit the Rocket Ships balls

PART 3: SMALL SIDED GAME (WITH A SLIGHT CHANGE)

With this part, simply return to the original small sided game that was set up for pre-practise. But now add in a slight change to the rules so that you are encouraging the children to work on a skill for this session.

For example, if you are teaching the children to dribble, make a goal worth 2 points if they run past a player and score.

Introduce this scoring system to encourage certain skills that you are focussing on and sportspersonship. But it still stays as a regular, fun game.

Here are 5 changes to implement in different training sessions:

CHANGE 1: REWARD TEAM PLAY - A goal is worth 2 points if a different player from the team scores the next goal.

CHANGE 2: REWARD DRIBBLING - A goal is worth 2 points if a player beats an opponent before scoring.

CHANGE 3: REWARD SKILL - A goal is worth 2 points if a player scores with their non-prefered foot.

CHANGE 4: REWARD DEFENDING - A player gets a high five (or a point for their team) if they stop an almost certain goal from the opposition.

CHANGE 5: REWARD SPORTSPERSONSHIP - A player gets a high five if they help another player up off the ground.

PART 4: FUN GAME

This Part focuses on developing children's basic skills and movement.

These games/drills are easy to implement for all skill levels and aim at improving players general movement plus give them confidence.

These Skill and Movement games can be for any number of players plus the players get to spend more time on the ball.

Here are 5 different exercises to use for Part 4 of your sessions:

FUN GAME
GAME #1
"ON YOUR TOES"

1. Split the players into two teams. Players each have a ball and dribble around in the middle section.

2. The coach calls out a colour of one of the teams. This team tries to get to the end zone and score in any goal.

3. The other team leaves their ball and tries to stop the other players.

WHAT TO FOCUS ON:
- Close ball control.
- Players should be listening and **on their toes ready to either score or defend.**

PROGRESSION:
#1. Can players use their non-preferred foot to score?

#2. Instead of calling out the colour, hold up a cone or bib of the colour of the team that is to get to the end zone. This way the children have to have their heads up and look around.

#3. Instead of calling out a colour, call out some letters. For example, "Players names starting with ABCDE!". This will keep them thinking.

#4. There is no Black or White end - players can try and dribble into either end zone and score.

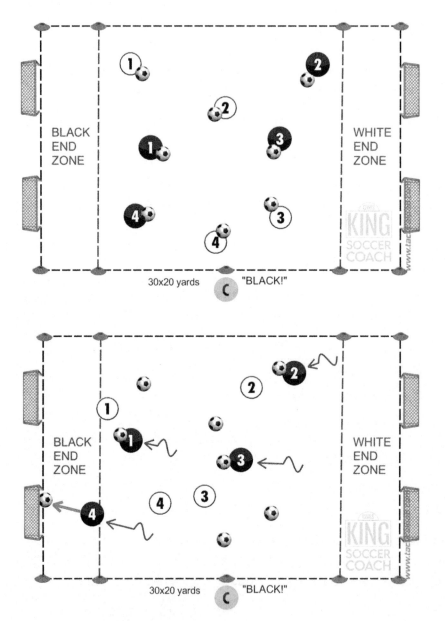

Summary of "On Your Toes" :

- All players dribble around the centre area.

- The coach calls out a colour of one team (Black in this case).

- All Black players try to get to their end zone and score in either goal.

- The White team leaves their ball and tries to stop the Blacks from scoring.

FUN GAME
GAME #2
"TAG"

1. Split the players into pairs with each pair having a colour (ie 1 blue pair, 1 red pair, 1 green pair, 1 yellow pair. If not enough bibs number them off in pairs instead).

2. All players have a ball and dribble around in the area.

3. The Coach calls out a colour and that colour is "it".

4. The "it" colour pair dribbles around for 30 seconds and try to tag any of the other players (touch any player with their hand) getting 1 point for each tag.

5. If any of the other players don't get tagged by the end they get 2 points.

6. Play the game until all pairs have been "it" and then add up the points. Give a free high five to the winners!

WHAT TO FOCUS ON:
1. Close control and changes of direction when dribbling.
2. Using all parts of their feet (inside, outside and sole).
3. Heads up and awareness of where the taggers are.
4. Make sure to look for the above 3 things and praise players as they do them!

PROGRESSION:
#1. Call out two colours to be "it" at once!

#2. Call out yourself! Then dribble around and get them all!

Watch them try extra hard to not get tagged by the coach.

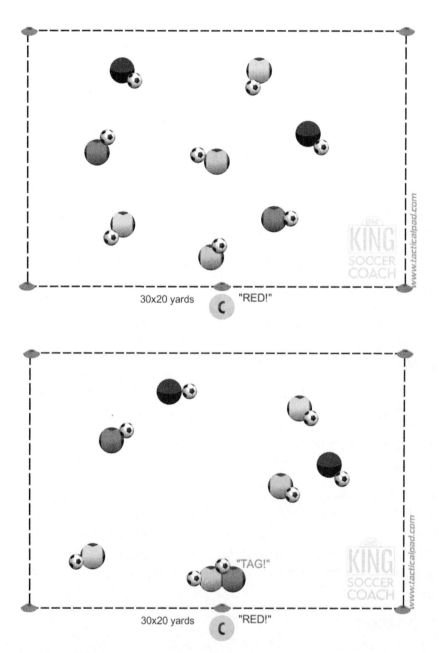

Summary of "Tag":

- Players are paired off in colours and then dribble around an area.

- The Coach calls out a colour (in this case "Red").

- The two Red players now became "it" and aim to tag as many others in 30 seconds as they can.

- They get 1 point for each tag and any player that doesn't get tagged receives 2 points.

FUN GAME
GAME #3
"BUDDY TAG"

1. Players are partnered up - one with a ball, one without (who is the Tagger!).

2. The player with the ball tries to keep away from the Tagger. If they get tagged they swap roles.

WHAT TO FOCUS ON:
- Dribbling at speed (but still under control).
- Good changes of direction to throw the tagger off.

PROGRESSION:
#1. Change every minute (count how many times each gets tagged)

#2. Make it so the Tagger has a ball and is dribbling as well

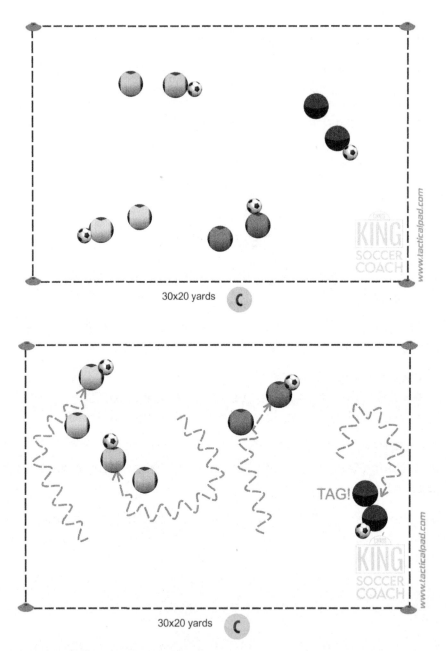

30x20 yards C

30x20 yards C

Summary of "Partner Tag" :

- One player from each pair starts dribbling with a ball.

- Their partner chases them and calls "Tag!" when they catch them.

- Swap roles when tagged (or alternatively each player dribbles for 1 minute and then swap and count up the Tags).

FUN GAME
GAME #4
"LITTLE, LITTLE, BIG!"

1. All players line up with a ball at one end of a small area - make sure to have some space between each player.

2. Then they dribble to the other side and as they dribble they kick the ball a short distance, another short one and then a big one! As they do this, they yell "Little! Little! Big!" in time with the kicks they are doing.

WHAT TO FOCUS ON:
- The parts of the foot they use - make sure they kick it as straight as they can and use the instep to pass the ball for the little kicks and then near their laces for the bigger kicks.

- Timing of their kicks - as they are running/dribbling with the ball it helps to teach them how to pass/kick on the run.

TIP:
If you have lots of players, make another line behind the first row and they can go as soon as the first row has had their second little kick.

PROGRESSION:
Can they use their non-preferred foot?

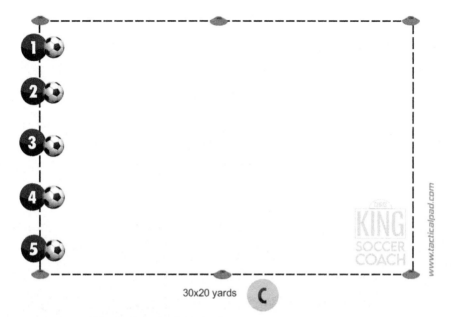

30x20 yards

Summary of "Little Little Big" :

- All the players line up at one end with a bit of space between each of them.

- They dribble out and have three kicks - the first two are little passes out in front and the third one is a big kick out in front.

- Get them to yell out "Little, Little, Big" as they kick.

FUN GAME
GAME #5
"CHICKEN"

1. Pair players off and start them facing each other about 15 yards apart with a ball each.

2. Players dribble at each other and just before they get to each other they do a turn/move to go back the other way.

3. Burst off and get back to where they started.

WHAT TO FOCUS ON:
- Timing of the move - make sure they don't do their move too early or too late.
- Use Pull Backs, L-Turns or Step Overs and Sole Rolls.

PROGRESSION:
#1. Instead of turning and going back, can the players do a move to get past each other? One player can take it in turns of calling out what move they should both do as they dribble towards each other.

#2 . Call out a number from one side and a different one from the other side so players swap and battle against a different opponent.

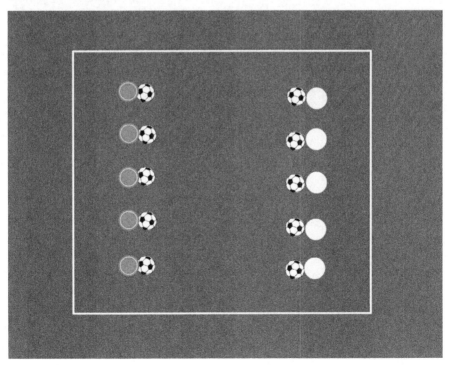

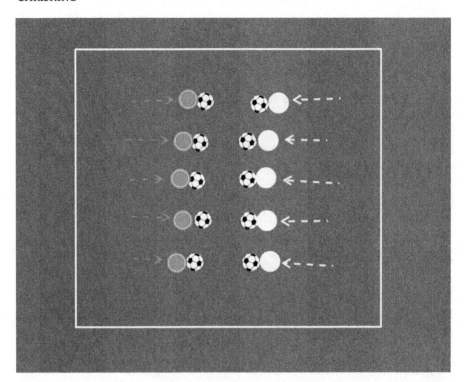

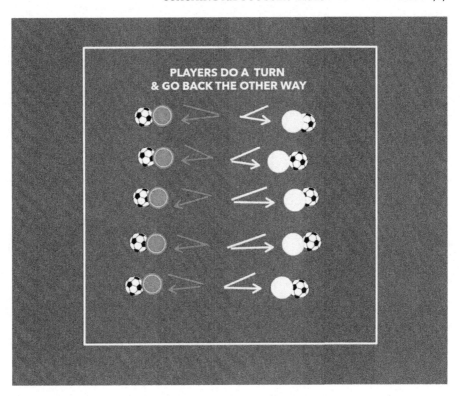

Summary of "Chicken" :

- Players partner up and line up opposite each other, both with a ball.

- On the coaches call, they dribble towards each other.

- Just before reaching each other players perform a turn/ trick and head off quickly the other way.

- **PROGRESSION:** Players do a 'trick/move' and go past the player instead of turning.

PART 5: SMALL SIDED GAME

This is the same as Part 3 "Small Sided Game: With a Slight Change". Let the kids finish with a game so they can enjoy themselves and try out anything new they've learnt from the session!

Just sit back, encourage and praise aspects of their game.

If you want to mix it up, feel free to put two goals at each end. This provides more scoring chances and therefore more opportunities for the children to experience success.

PART 2
ESSENTIAL SOCCER SKILLS

"Put in the time and work developing your skills now - and thank yourself later!"
Chris King

Like most new skills, the best way to learn them is to **start slowly, learn them correctly** and then speed up as you become more familiar and confident. So make sure your players:

- **Start slow and stay patient!**
- **Work hard!**
- **Spend time practising at home!**
- **Repeat, repeat, repeat the skill!**

5 to 10 year olds can be like border collies when they enjoy something - obsessive! Once they see a new skill or trick they will do it over and over. If you can show them the initial skills and create a fun learning environment, they will have the time to improve and master these skills.

They can practise at home, view YouTube tutorials and play with their friends or parents and improve immensely. So don't underestimate your role in fanning the flame that may become a life filled with fitness, friends and fun.

Let's start with some "Essential Soccer Skills" and then we can move on to other skills further on in the book.

1. GETTING USED TO THE BALL: Toe Taps; Sole Rolls

2. **TURNS:** Drag Back; L-Turn

3. **DRIBBLING:** How To Dribble: Inside Out

4. **BEAT A PLAYER:** Inside Chop; Double Step Over

1. GETTING USED TO THE BALL

These skills will lead to confidence on the ball and the players will be able to develop ball control. It's all about getting the players to have as many touches on the ball as possible! All parts of the foot should be used.

Always start slowly with each new skill. Work on getting the correct technique and then build up to moving quicker once they have gained confidence.

TOE TAPS

Toe Taps are simply touches on the top of the ball using the sole of the boot. They help improve coordination, improve players quickness of feet and improve their touch on the ball.

How to do Toe Taps:
The player should stand with the ball directly in front of them.

Now they put the sole of one foot on top of the ball while keeping the other one planted on the ground.

Then switch feet so the opposite sole of the foot is on the ball and the other foot is on the ground. Repeat this.

Players should go as slowly as required to start with. Eventually they will be doing it in a fluid motion. Build up so that eventually players will be "bouncing" (moving one foot as soon as the other touches the top of the ball).

Key points to remember:

- Use the bottom of the boot where your toes meet the ball of your foot to tap the ball
- Nice and soft (don't stomp on the ball!)
- Find balance and keep the head over the ball

Progression for Toe Taps:

1. SPINNING - Keep the ball in the one spot, but move to the left and right around the ball while doing Toe Taps (ie the body will move but the ball stays stationary).

2. FORWARD AND BACKWARDS - With the sole of the feet, players softly push the ball forward for a few touches. Then softly pull the ball backwards with the sole of the feet.

3. FIGURE 8 - Place two cones approximately 3 metres apart. Now moving forward (or backwards) do Toe Taps in a figure 8 shape around the cones.

TOE TAPS

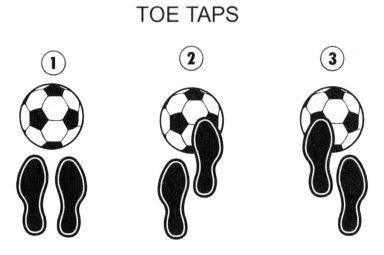

IMAGE - TOE TAPS:
1 - Start with both feet behind the ball.

2 - Keep the left foot on the ground and raise the right foot and gently tap the top of the ball with your toes.

3 - Swap feet so the left toe taps the ball and the right foot returns to the ground.

SOLE ROLLS

This helps with players' touch and learning to move the ball.

How to do Sole Rolls:

Simply roll the ball softly **with the sole of the foot** in any direction. Then, with the same foot, roll it back to the starting position. For example, roll it out to the right with the sole of the right foot, then roll it back to the starting position with the sole of the right foot.

Start by doing it in the one spot and then progress to moving around the ground doing it.

Once they have the hang of it, players can roll it forward, backwards or whichever direction they want with the sole of either foot.

And once they are comfortable, get them to alternate feet - so it might be to roll it out to the right with your right foot, then roll it out to the left with the left foot.

TIP: Tell the kids to do it at home while sitting on the couch, walking around the house or walking home from school! (Maybe buy a soft soccer ball in case they get carried away at home).

SOLE ROLLS

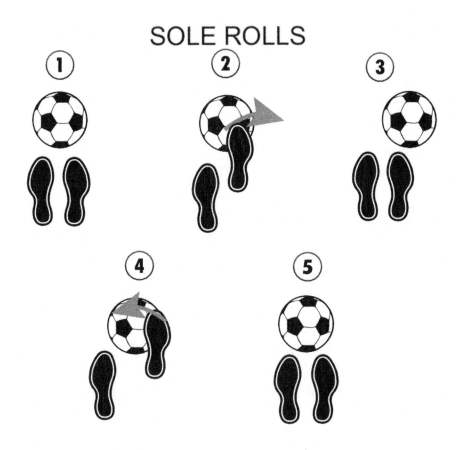

IMAGE - SOLE ROLLS:

1 - Start with both feet behind the ball (the same starting position as Toe Taps).

2 - Roll the ball to the right with the sole of the right foot.

3 - The ball should finish slightly out to the right of the body as in the above image.

4 - Now roll the ball back to the starting position with the same foot (right foot).

5 - The ball should finish in its original starting position.

2. TURNS

Every footballer should have a couple of turns in their locker!

They help the player to turn away from a defender or disguise their intentions.

Turns also help young players with spacial awareness, keeping close control and getting out of a tight situation. And this in turn (pun intended) all helps the player and team keep possession.

DRAG BACK

The Drag Back will help players change direction quickly and they will also learn to protect the ball.

How To Do A Drag Back:

Put one foot to the side of the ball. Place the other foot on top of the ball (similar to as if the player was going to do a Sole Roll), then roll it straight back behind and move off in the other direction.

The body should turn in the same direction as the foot that is being used. For example, if the player is dragging the ball back with their right foot, their right shoulder and the rest of their body should turn so they end up facing 180 degrees in the other direction.

Get players to try with one foot for 30 seconds and then swap to use the other foot for 30 seconds.

A good activity to get players using the drag back once they are used to it is "Chicken". Simply get them all in a square and get players to dribble at each other and then do a drag back just as they get to each other and dribble off in the other direction and find someone else to dribble at! This will get them used to timing the drag back and doing it under pressure.

Another good one (I call it "Quick Draw") is to get them to partner up and stand on either side of a ball jogging on the spot. The coach yells "Pull!" and the first player to react pulls the ball back and dribbles off with the other player trying to win it back. Stop and reset after 15-20 seconds.

112

DRAG BACK

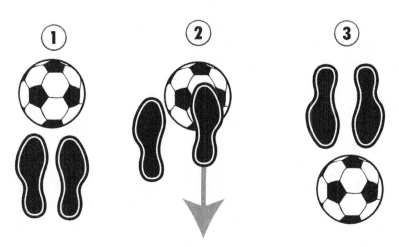

IMAGE - DRAG BACK:

1 - Start with both feet behind the ball.

2 - Place the left foot beside the ball and the sole of the right foot on the ball (just like a Sole Roll or Toe Tap). Roll it directly back behind you. Turn your body as you do it (if it's your right foot, your right shoulder and the rest of your body should turn to the right as you drag the ball back).

3 - You should end up facing 180 degrees in the other direction and in a game situation, the player can then protect the ball or dribble off.

L-TURN

Amazingly, this turn is called the L-Turn as the ball moves in an L shape direction. The L-Turn will help players change direction quickly and move the ball out of the opposition's grasp. (If you are familiar with the Cruyff turn it is similar to that).

How To Do An L-Turn:

Similar to the Drag Back, put one foot to the side of the ball. Place the other foot on top of the ball (similar to attempting a Sole Roll), roll it backwards and touch/push it behind the planted foot using the instep of the foot (it goes in an 'L' shape behind the planted foot).

Once they have got the hang of this, the player can stop the ball by putting the left foot on top of the ball once it goes behind and turns away in the left direction.

The player should end up facing approximately 90 degrees to the left or right (depending which foot you have used).

The same as the Drag Back, a good activity to get players using the L-Turn is "Chicken". Simply get them all in a square and get players to dribble at each other and then do an L-Turn just as they get to each other and dribble off in the other direction. This will get them used to timing the pull back to start the L-Turn and doing it under pressure.

L-TURN

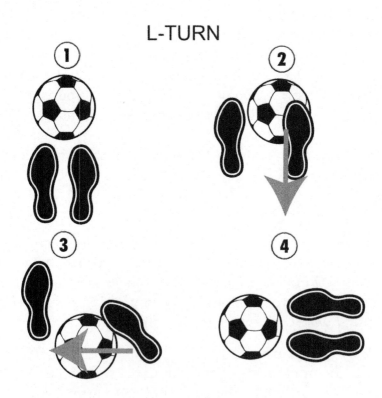

IMAGE - L-TURN:
1 - Start with both feet behind the ball.
2 - Place the left foot next to the ball and place the sole of the right foot on top of the ball and drag it backwards.
3 - As it rolls, now use the instep of the right foot to move it behind the left foot.
4 - The body should turn to the left and the ball will be in front of the player who can then shield it or dribble off.

3. DRIBBLING

It's all well and good to be able to do skills while standing in the one spot but during the game you need to get a move on! So let's start dribbling.

The aim when dribbling is to move the ball quickly while keeping it close to the body. This is so that an opposition player can't steal it and so that the dribbler can make a quick decision to either pass, shoot or change direction.

Here's how to dribble *plus* an extra move to use while dribbling (once the player has become comfortable).

the DRIBBLE
Use the inside and outside of the front of the boot

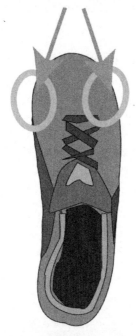

The inside should be near where the big toe meets the foot

The outside should be near where the little toe meets the foot

INSIDE + OUTSIDE OF THE FOOT DRIBBLING

This helps with the players touch and feel for the ball on the outside and inside of their boot plus it improves change of direction when dribbling.

How To Do Inside + Outside of the Foot Dribbling:

Use just one foot to start with: With the ball in front of one foot, touch it forward with the front inside of that foot, follow the ball and touch it forward with the front outside of the same foot. Do this for 5 metres and then switch to using the other foot.

Make sure to keep the ball close - don't just kick and chase otherwise an opponent will steal it!

Please note: The player should point their toes downwards slightly when using the outside of their foot.

INSIDE/OUTSIDE DRIBBLING

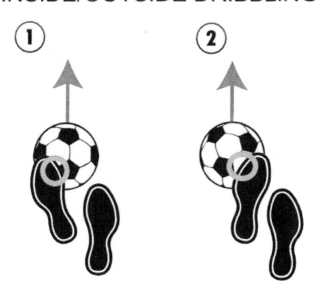

IMAGE - INSIDE/OUTSIDE DRIBBLING:

1 - Start with pushing the ball forward with the inside of the left foot (where the green circle is). Push the ball halfway up the ball. Then step forward with the right foot.

2 - Now push the ball forward with the outstep of the left foot (where the green circle is). Remember to point the toes slightly downwards. Then take a step forward with the right foot.

3 - Repeat this sequence and get faster as players improve (the players should be just walking as they first learn to dribble).

RUNNING AND DRIBBLING

This type of dribbling is used when there is space in front and the player wants to get a bit of speed up.

How To Do Running and Dribbling:

While running in a straight line, **push the ball with the outside of the boot** (see green circle in the image). The shape of the foot should be toes pointed down and facing slightly inward. This helps to keep the natural running motion and keeps speed up (if the player were to dribble with their toes pointed out, this would slow them down and they would run like a duck).

When starting out, just walk or lightly jog and keep the ball one step in front. Use one foot to push the ball (i.e. push with right foot, step with left foot, push with right foot, step with left foot).

PROGRESSION: As they improve and start running, push the ball a little further in front and they can take 2 or 3 steps in between each touch but make sure to not just kick and chase the ball!

RUNNING & DRIBBLING

IMAGE - RUNNING AND DRIBBLING:

1 - Start with pushing the ball forward with the outside of your right foot (where the green circle is). Then take one step forward with the left foot.

2 - Do exactly the same again (push the ball with the outside of the right foot).

3 - Eventually as players get better they should be taking 2 or 3 steps in between each touch.

Once they've mastered the basics of dribbling, why not add in some turns that they learnt earlier? Dribble and then every 5 or 10 seconds do a Drag Back or L-Turn. Or even just simply change direction and explode off like a rocket going to space! Change of speed can be key to losing a defender.

4. BEAT A PLAYER

One v One situations occur frequently in football. So from an early age, it is important to teach children how to get past an opponent. They can then take these skills away to practise and develop them on their own or with friends. That's the great thing about football! All you need is a ball, some spare time and you will improve.

Being able to take on and dribble past an opponent will give the players confidence, so here are some skills to help them on their footballing journey.

As always, get players to start off very slowly until they start to grasp the skill.

SHOULDER DROP + INSIDE CHOP

Once perfected, this can be done at pace and should send the defender the wrong way to give you a couple of yards of space to dribble off to the other side.

How To Do Shoulder Drop + Inside Chop:
1. Dribble towards a player/cone.
2. Just before you reach them, drop the shoulder in the direction you want to send the defender (i.e. drop the right shoulder to send them to your right).
3. Now with the inside of the right foot 'chop' (come down on the side of the ball quickly) the outside of the ball so it comes back across in front of the body and dribble away to the left.
4. Note: The chop should be done as soon as the shoulder is dropped - almost in one motion.

SHOULDER DROP +
INSIDE CHOP

Once youve dropped the shoulder use the inside part of the boot to chop down on the ball so it goes across your body

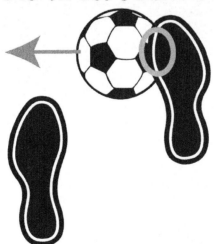

DOUBLE STEP OVER

Start off learning this skill stationary and build up to dribbling at a player and performing it. It will leave them guessing which way you are going to go!

Note: **Start with just a single step over and build up to the double.**

the STEP OVER
the right foot goes in and around the ball (clockwise direction)

How To Do Double Step Over:

1. Dribble towards a player/cone.

2. Circle one foot around the ball - start on the inside of the ball, circle up and to the outside and back (if the **right foot is being used the foot should be going clockwise** around the ball. If using the **left foot it should be going anti-clockwise**).

3. Circle the other foot around from the inside to outside and back.

4. Take off in the direction of your first step over. (ie if you used your right foot for the first step over head off to the right). Do this by pushing the ball with the outside of your foot. I.e. If you want to head off in the right direction, push the ball to the right after the step overs. So the sequence will be: Step over; step over; push the ball.

End of "ESSENTIAL SKILLS" section

PART 3
FURTHER SOCCER SKILLS

"Don't be a one trick player - have a few different moves and learn to use both feet at a young age so you keep the opposition guessing. Also, in soccer and life, you might be down at one stage, but if you never give up, you'll be back on top because hard work pays off."
Chris King

Once the player has learnt some of the basics and is ready to move on they can add these skills below.

And remember to **always start slowly with each new skill**. Work on getting the correct technique and then build up to going quicker. Good work coach!

These are some more skills you will be teaching your players:

1. BALL CONTROL

- Happy Feet
- Inside and Outside of Feet
- Push and Pull
- Triangles
- Squares

2. PASSING AND CONTROLLING

- Push Pass
- Laces Pass (also known as Instep Drive)
- Basic Receiving Skills

3. JUGGLING

- Juggling Basics
- Foot Surfaces Juggling Challenge
- Heights Juggling Challenge

1. BALL CONTROL

HAPPY FEET

Happy feet are when the player is tapping the ball back and forth between the inside of their feet. Use the instep of both feet and tap it back and forth. Think of it like that old computer game "Pong".

This helps with players' touch on the ball, coordination and quick feet.

How To Do Happy Feet:
1. Start slow jogging on the spot
2. Step up to the ball and have it between the feet
3. While still slowly jogging on the spot, lightly tap the ball with the inside of your feet so the ball goes from the left foot to the right foot and back again, continuously.

Tips: Keep the head over the ball, be light on the feet and as always, start slowly until the player gets used to it.

Progression for Happy Feet:
1. Do Happy Feet while **turning to the left or right**
2. Do Happy Feet while **moving forward and backwards**

3. Do Happy Feet while **moving sideways**

4. Do Happy Feet and **stop it with the sole of your foot** every 5th tap then continue on

HAPPY FEET
use the inner part of both feet to tap the ball back and forth

Think of it like the old computer game Pong. This Skill really helps with touch and coordination

INSIDE CHOP AND PUSH

This helps a player move the ball quickly away from a defender. The defender may think they have a chance to win the ball but the player chops the ball with one foot and moves it further away with the other. Use this move to quickly change direction and dribble off.

When I use the term 'chop' or 'cut', I am referring to a quick, sudden movement with the foot which makes the ball move in a different direction. So, for example, you would chop the outside of the ball with the inside of your right foot to quickly move the ball to the left.

How To Do Inside Chop & Push:

1. Start off learning this one while stationary. Then, when there is improvement, practise it while dribbling

2. Chop the outside of the ball with the right foot so the ball comes across the body (right to left)

3. Next use the outside of the left foot to push the ball further to the left

So the rhythm should be: chop with the right, push with the outside of the left

4. Then back the other way: chop with the left, push with the outside of the right foot

INSIDE CHOP AND PUSH

1. use the inner part of the foot to chop down on the ball so it goes across your body

INSIDE CHOP AND PUSH

2. as the ball comes across the body push it further to the left with your left foot

PUSH AND PULL

This push and pull technique is great for touch and close control. Plus it can be done in any small area.

All it consists of is the player, on the spot, pushing the ball forward with the front of one foot and then pulling it back with the sole of the other foot.

How To Do Push and Pull:
1. Push the ball forward with the top (front part of the top of the boot) of the right foot so it goes in front of your left foot
2. Pull the ball back to your body with the sole of your left foot
3. Push the ball back out with the top of the left foot ((front part of the top of the boot) so it goes in front of your right foot
4. Pull the ball back to your body with the sole of the right foot
Repeat the sequence

PUSH AND PULL
1. use the top outer part of the foot to push the ball out on a slight angle across the body

PUSH AND PULL

2. now use the sole of the left foot to pull the ball back in to the body. Then repeat back the other way

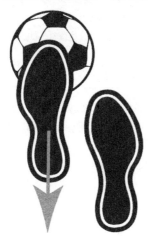

TRIANGLES

This drill builds from the Push and Pull and helps with touch, fast feet and ball control. It is simply moving the ball in a triangular pattern in front of the body using the soles and/or outside of the feet.

How To Do Triangles:

1. Start with feet slightly apart and the ball in front of the body
2. Pull the ball backwards towards the body with the sole of the right foot

4. Push the ball forward with the sole, inside or outside of the left foot to its starting position (this should have completed the triangle shape)
Repeat

Note: To make things harder, you can place a cone in front of the player so they can do the Triangle around it without touching it

Progression for Triangles:
1. For more advanced players that have mastered this, get them to use the one foot for all three touches. They will be hopping on one foot to adjust their body while using the sole of their other foot to move the ball in the triangular shape.

SQUARES

The next move up from Triangles is of course Squares. This adds in another touch to make the triangle into a square to improve a player's close control.

How To Do Squares:
1. Push the ball straight forward with the right foot
2. Still with the right foot (use the instep or sole), touch/roll the ball across the body to the left
3. Pull the ball back in towards the body with the sole of the left foot
4. Push the ball back across the body with the left foot (use the instep or sole) to the right to complete the square shape
5. Repeat

Note: To make things harder, you can place a cone in front of the player so they can do the Square around it without touching it

2. PASSING AND CONTROLLING

Pele, Maradona, Baggio, Bergkamp, Messi and Ronaldo didn't magically start doing 40 yard pin point passes and controlling the ball instantly. They all started with the basics of passing and controlling a ball, then did it a zillion times to improve (if you want to see what repetition can do for a players hand-eye coordination, go to YouTube and type "Bradman golf ball and stump" to see how the best cricket to ever play the game worked on his batting skills growing up).

Growing up, when I was indoors I used to pass it against the back of my couch 1000 times or when outside against a wall - pass, control, pass, control, pass, control. When inside I would put on my favourite CD (usually Beastie Boys, Beatles or Sigue Sigue Sputnik) and pass and control until it finished. You can get a lot of repetition in this way and improve at a great rate. All you need is something like a couch, a wall, a bench turned on its side, etc.

But I'm getting ahead of myself - firstly, how do you pass a ball?

The best and most accurate pass to start with is using the inside (or instep - i.e. where the Nike Swoosh would be on the inside of the boot) of your foot - we call this the Push Pass. The instep is a large area and can generate power. So for short to medium distance passing, let's go with the inside of the foot (which I shall refer to as the instep from now on).

the SOCCER BOOT

the TOP OF THE BOOT
(used for laces pass)

the INSTEP
(used for the push pass)

PUSH PASS

The main aspects of the Push Pass are:

1. Aim with the non kicking foot
2. Open the hip up
3. Body (shoulders and head) over the ball
4. Lock the ankle
5. Hit the middle of the ball with the instep

1. Aim with the non-kicking foot

The ball should be slightly in front of the body, not stuck under the body. It should be at a slight angle to the body as well, not directly in front otherwise the heel of the foot will kick the ball and the other foot will get in the way.

So, for example, **if kicking the ball with the right foot, the ball should be slightly in front of the body at the 1 o'clock position**. Glance at the target and then look back at the ball (this helps with aiming but also to see if the other player is ready to receive the ball!).

Next, step to the ball (this can be a couple of short steps) and **plant the non-passing foot next to the ball**. Make sure to aim the non-passing foot at the target.

Key points to remember when stepping to the ball are:
- Bend the knee and point the toes of your non-passing foot towards the target.
- **Don't lean back!** The head should be over the chest.
- Don't stop completely before striking the ball - it should be fluid.

2. Open The Hip Up
The hip of the passing leg should open up as the leg is taken back. This allows the player to hit the ball with the instep of the foot with a nice open and flat contact which will send the ball straight. Try to make sure the foot is at a 90 degree angle to the planted foot.

3. Body over the ball
With the Push Pass, we want to do it along the ground so it is easy for our teammate to control. Therefore we **don't want to be leaning back** which may lead to getting under the ball. Also make sure players aren't reaching for the ball, as this won't generate enough power.

Players want to have their body (shoulders and head) over the ball. This will generate power and allow them to hit the ball in the middle of the ball and not lift it off the ground.

4. Lock the ankle

Older players most likely lock the ankle subconsciously when striking/passing a ball. But as a child learning the technique, they should be reminded to lock their ankle when they strike the ball.

To lock the ankle when doing a Push Pass, simply think of pulling the toes up and rotating them out slightly. This should create a solid ankle and they can strike the ball with good control (as the ankle won't move when hitting the ball and therefore not allowing the pass to go wayward) and good power.

5. Hit the middle of the ball

We want to be striking the ball in the centre/middle of the ball when doing a Push Pass. This will create a firm pass and the ball will travel on the ground. If the ball is struck under the middle of the ball it will lift the ball. If struck above the middle, it will go into the ground and not go very far.

So try to get the players to look at the middle of the ball as they are striking the ball and aim for that part of the ball.

Summary

Some key points to remember when doing a Push Pass are:
- Aim at the target with the planted foot
- Rotate the hip of the kicking foot to open up the instep of the foot and create a 90 degree angle with the planted foot
- Don't lean back! **Step into the ball** and have the body over the ball
- Just before striking the ball, lock the ankle for maximum power and accuracy
- Hit the middle of the ball so it goes along the ground

IMAGE - PUSH PASS:
1 - Plant the non-kicking foot next to the ball. Aim at the target with the planted foot
2- The kicking foot is similar to a pendulum - the hip opens up and the leg swings backwards
3 - Step into the ball with the ankle locked and hit the ball in the centre of the ball so it travels along the ground
4 - Follow through in the direction you want the ball to travel

LACES PASS (OR INSTEP DRIVE)

Once players have got used to the Push Pass, they can move onto the Laces Pass - also called the Instep Drive.

The Laces Pass uses a different part of the foot and strikes the ball in a different area.

We want to strike the ball under the middle of the ball so the ball goes in the air. And we want to strike it near or with the laces of your boot (refer to "the Soccer Boot" image a couple of pages back to see what part of the boot to use).

Here is the Laces Pass broken into 4 parts...

A) WHICH PART OF THE FOOT TO USE TO STRIKE THE BALL
The best way to show children which part of the foot is to sit them down and point out the large bone that runs along the top of the foot.

Then get them all to grab a ball, do a little throw in the air and as it comes down try and kick it with the laces area that the big bone in the foot runs along.

Once they have grasped which part of the foot they want to be using, place the balls on the ground.

B) WHICH PART OF THE BALL TO STRIKE
You want to be striking **slightly under the centre of the ball.**

This will create some loft (the lower down on the ball you strike, the higher the ball will go).

C)THE APPROACH AND STRIKE
Players should start around 3 steps back from the ball and they want to **approach the ball at approximately a 30-40 degree angle**.

If a player is striking the ball with their right foot they want to be stepping like this:
Left, Right, Left (plant the Left next to the ball) and then strike with the Right.

As the non-kicking leg is planted (the Left), the Right foot is drawn back.

The ankle should be locked with the toes pointed slightly down. Both knees should be bent and the bent knee of the kicking leg should be almost over the ball.

The planted foot should be beside the ball but not too close! If the planted foot is really close to the ball it will feel unnatural and the kicking foot won't have any room to come in at an angle. Get the players to experiment and see what feels comfortable to them.

D) THE FOLLOW THROUGH
After striking the ball, players must follow through to get the maximum power on the pass. **If it's a short pass they won't have to follow through as far.** If they want to try and pass all the way across the pitch they may have to follow through as far as they can.

An example of this in another sport is golf. When you see a golfer tee off (usually looking to get maximum distance) they take a big backswing and they follow through all the way. They don't just hit the ball and stop the club dead. So when doing a big kick in soccer, **follow through to get more distance.**

And when golfers are doing a nice little chip from just off the green they will do a small backswing and a small follow through so they can control it better and land it closer. The same when doing a shorter Laces Pass, don't take as big a swing or follow through.

TRY NOT TO...
These may be some of the issues that are affecting the execution of the Laces Pass:

- Balls flying off course: Get the players to make sure they lock their ankles (encourage them to point their toes down). Also make sure they are hitting just below the middle of the ball;
- Planted foot facing in the wrong direction.
- No power: The planted foot may be too far from the ball; or the initial swing or follow through may not be big enough.

IMAGE - LACES STRIKE:

1 - Start a few steps back and approach the ball at a 30-40 degree angle. Then as the player arrives at the ball, plant the non-kicking foot beside the ball (not too close to it - we want to allow enough room for the other leg and foot to swing through)

2 - The kicking leg should be bent back ready to strike down and through the ball

3 - Aim to strike just under the centre of the ball with the lower part of your laces where the bone runs along the top of the foot

4 - Follow through for more power

CONTROLLING

Next we'll learn how to control a pass (also called your first touch or trapping a ball).

The best way to learn how to control a ball is to either pass back and forth with a partner or find a wall or bench that they can pass against. If a player wants to practise inside, they could get a soft soccer ball and pass off a wall inside. And if the parents or friend can't pass a ball with their feet, they can always throw it along the ground to them.

As always, players should start off slowly. So make sure that it is just a soft, slow pass to the child so that they can master the basic points before trying to receive balls coming at pace.

And before we really get into it, always remember USE BOTH FEET! If kids start now it will be a great asset throughout their whole football journey.

Okay here we go - let's start with passing a ball off a wall (or to another player) and then I will give the 6 key points that will improve the control.

Pass the ball off the wall and as it comes back, **use a soft touch with the instep of the foot** to control the ball. Then pass the ball back into the wall and repeat the control as it comes back.

6 KEY POINTS WHEN CONTROLLING THE BALL

1. IMAGINE CATCHING AN EGG: Players should cushion/cradle the ball with the instep of the foot to take the pace off. So imagine if they were catching an egg with their hands. They would take their hands down with the speed of the egg. So they want to do the same with the instep of the foot when they trap/control the soccer ball. Don't be rigid and hard, **be relaxed and let the foot go back with the ball.**

2. MEET THE BALL IN FRONT OF THE BODY: Have the foot slightly out in front of the planted foot to make room to cushion the ball back in. And don't wait until the ball has hit the foot before they start cushioning it in - **start moving the foot back JUST BEFORE the ball hits the foot.** Timing is key here so don't expect to get it straight away (remember **Practice! Practice! Practice!** and before you know it it will be second nature).

3. MAKE CONTACT WITH THE MIDDLE OF THE BALL: This should go without saying but for the ball to stay in front of the body, control it on the middle of the ball. This is handy to know for the future. Because as children progress and try different types of control, if the ball was coming in the air they would have to raise their leg higher and make contact *above* the middle of the ball to bring it down. Or underneath the ball to make it go up.

4. SLIGHTLY LEAN FORWARD: As the ball comes to the player, they should have a slight lean forward in their chest and that way they can lean back with the ball when it makes contact which helps with the cushioning.

5. KEEP YOUR EYE ON THE BALL: This is key so you can read the pace of the ball and focus on when to start bringing your foot back. It also helps in case the ball bobbles or moves just before it reaches you so you can adjust.

6. THE BALL SHOULD FINISH SLIGHTLY IN FRONT: When you finish the control of the ball, it should be slightly in front of you. This way you can make the next pass without the ball being stuck under your body.

Also when controlling a ball, try not to stretch for the ball out to the side of the body - move the whole body instead so the ball is in front which will make it easier to control. Quick feet! Be on your toes!

3. JUGGLING

In soccer, juggling is simply the act of keeping the soccer ball in the air using any part of your body (except for your arms and hands).

And juggling is a key part of any soccer player aiming to improve their touch, control and coordination. Plus it can be done by yourself, virtually anywhere!

Why learn to juggle? Well during a game balls will be coming at all different heights and angles, so players will need to be able to control a ball at any height or angle with different parts of their body.

It's not easy to start with but with a bit of patience and practise it will be worth it once players start controlling balls during a game with ease.

BOUNCE JUGGLING (BEGINNERS)

Kids don't want to become frustrated when first learning anything, so bounce juggling is a great way for players to get used to juggling without feeling like it's too hard.

It's simply allowing the ball to bounce in between every juggle (touch) which allows them to position their body ready for the next juggle without feeling rushed.

HOW TO BOUNCE JUGGLE

1. Pick up the ball using the hands and gentle throw it in the air at chest height, slightly out from the body
2. Let the ball bounce and start to get the body in position and the foot ready to take a juggle touch
3. Once the ball starts moving down and gets to about knee/shin

height, take a touch using the top of the boot

4. Try to kick the ball to chest/head height. This will allow enough time to get ready for the next touch (as they progress and improve they should aim to mostly kick the ball lower)

5. Get balanced so they are ready for the next touch. Let the ball bounce and then repeat!

6. Make sure to use both feet and progress to using thighs, chest and head once used to juggling with just the feet

Note: As players get more comfortable, only let the ball bounce every second juggle instead of every time. So it would be:
Throw; Bounce; Juggle; Bounce; Juggle; Juggle, Bounce; Juggle; Bounce; Juggle; Juggle and so on.

NO BOUNCE JUGGLING

Once players have become somewhat confident with Bounce Juggling, it's time to move on to No Bounce Juggling. Simply remove the bounce from the last stage. Here we go...

1. Pick the ball up but instead of throwing it up, gentle drop it to either foot

2. Once the ball starts moving down and gets to about knee/shin height take a touch using the top area of the boot

3. Try to kick the ball to chest/head height. This will allow enough time to get ready for the next touch (as players progress and improve they should aim to kick the ball lower)

4. Get balanced so they are ready for the next touch and juggle the ball again

5. Make sure to use both feet and progress to using thighs, chest and head once used to juggling with just the feet

Juggling can also be done with a partner and it can be great fun! They can either do it Bounce or No Bounce depending on the skill level. They can set competitions and get the kids to try and break their own record or juggle for 2 minutes and see which couple gets the most.

BONUS TIP

It can be a slow process picking the ball up each time you want to juggle. Plus it doesn't improve your foot skills. So if you want to show your kids how to do a "Kick Up" (a movement that gets the ball in the air so they can start juggling) I'm sure they'll master it after a bit. It does involve quick reactions and movements so make sure they stay patient. Here are the easiest two Kick Ups that I've come across:

ROLL BACK KICK UP:

1. Start with the ball one step in front. Use the sole of the preferred foot to drag the ball back towards the body
2. In one quick motion, place the same foot on the ground behind the rolling ball with the toes down like a ramp so the ball can roll up the foot
3. Once the ball reaches the toes or laces flick it up and start juggling! Yes get in!!!

THE HOP KICK UP

1. Start with the ball trapped between the feet (push the feet together so it creates pressure on the ball from both sides)
2. Now simply do a two footed hop up in the air to lift the ball and let it go
3. Land and start juggling as the ball comes down! Easy! Easy!

HERE IS A SKILL COACHING DRILL
FOR KIDS TO PRACTISE WHAT
THEY'VE JUST LEARNT

COACHING DRILL: "AROUND THE WORLD"

- This is a good drill to practise all the skills the players have learnt
- Set up a circle with cones spread evenly around the circle every 8 yards
- Players start on a cone with a ball each
- On the coaches call the players move to the right and

perform an essential skill. For example, the coach may say "Toe Taps!" so each player moves to the right doing toe taps on the ball until they reach the next cone

PROGRESSION:

Instead of going from cone to cone, players can stay on the one cone and perform the skill on the spot or around the cone

COACHES TIP:

- Players will be at different speeds and skill levels so anyone that finishes first can keep doing the skill at the next cone until everyone is ready

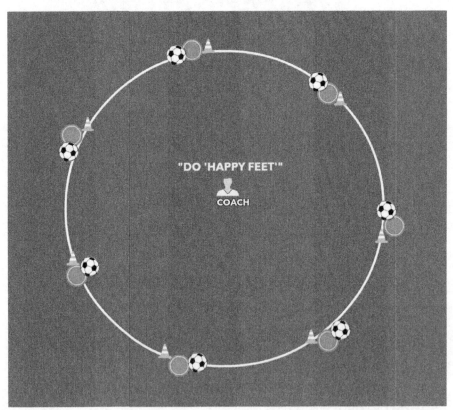

7 TIPS TO KEEP KIDS FOCUSSED

"There will usually be a couple of hyper, naughty kids in each session. Maybe that kid was you back in school? So make sure to learn some tips so you don't let them derail your training session."
Chris King

Kids are kids - they're hyper and they have the attention span of a gnat. So instead of getting frustrated, be prepared!

You may only have them for 30-40 minutes each week so we don't want to waste that valuable time.

Here are a few tips on how to keep kids focussed at soccer training...

1. KEEP YOUR TALKS SHORT!

To a certain extent this can relate to older players as well. **Soccer players come to training to play soccer, not listen to the coach yabber on.** So don't bore players with a long, detailed explanation of a drill. Give them a short description of the main points and get into the drill!

If you give them 10 different things to remember at the start it's a waste of everyone's time.

Once you've been going for a couple of minutes then you can stop and adjust it quickly and give them any more instructions. Or even just give instructions to a player who hasn't grasped it as the drill is going so that you're not constantly stopping it.

Players will enjoy it more and will take more information in.

2. KEEP THINGS MOVING!

Hands up who likes to stand in a line and wait? I thought so. So why make kids wait in line when they could be getting in more repetitions of the skill?

Instead of having long lines or kids waiting to come on, do this:

Set up multiple versions of the same drill side by side (I call it having a Mirror Drill). It stops the long wait in lines and therefore stops players getting bored and creating trouble. If you set the drills up side by side you can be in the middle and keep an eye on everything.

3. KEY SIGNALS

Getting kids' attention can be hard. Here are three Key Signals which help in getting your players attention!

1. One of my fellow coaches says **"Eyes!"** to his group of young players. It's amazing to watch, it's like he's a magician.

As soon as he says "Eyes!" his players know to stop what they are doing, if they have a ball sit on it and make eye contact with him. It's simple but very effective. If they are sitting on the ball they aren't kicking or bouncing it. And if they are looking at him he knows they are paying attention.

2. Another fun one is to say "Soccer Pose!". This is where your players stop what they're doing, put one foot on top of the soccer ball, fold their arms across their chest, turn their heads slightly to the side and look at you as if they're the best soccer player in the world. Kids love it! And it achieves the same as the "Eyes" - all players stop and look at you.

3. A third one is to say "Knee, Shoulders, Heads!". Players know to stop what they're doing and place their hands firstly on their knees, then shoulders and then head. This one works well because no one wants to be the last to put their hands on their head.

4. ASK QUESTIONS AS WELL AS SHOWING AND TELLING

This simply means when explaining a drill or skill, **phrase some sentences as a question** so the players are more involved.

An example would be if you're explaining how to do "Happy Feet" (quickly moving the ball back and forth between your feet), ask the group "What does a good 'Happy Feet' look like?" and then whoever puts their hands up, get them to show the group.

Even getting the kids to choose which drill they want to do to practise a particular skill will keep them engaged. Plus you get to see what type of drills they like.

An example of this would be if you were focussing on passing, ask the group "What game can we play that will help us with our passing?" And they may say "Gates!" (passing in pairs between cones spread around an area. This drill is in my first kids book "Coaching Kids Soccer Volume 1". Search for it on Amazon or go to my website www.chriskingsoccercoach.com if you want to grab a copy!). So you can quickly set it up while they pass between each other and away you go.

5. MAKE IT COMPETITIVE

This doesn't mean that there is a winner or loser each time. It may just be competing against how many passes/juggles/turns in a row they got the first time. Or how many Toe Taps they can do in 30 seconds.

Or as a group say "Let's see if we can all get 5 juggles!" - the better players can aim for 5 and go beyond it and the less skilled can try their best to get 5.

6. ACT LIKE YOU'VE HAD 3 CANS OF ENERGY DRINK AND JOIN IN

This is your chance to act stupid and keep the kids engaged! **Wave your arms around, bring lots of energy, be animated!** Be that crazy uncle or aunty that your nieces love! :) Give players high fives (down low too slow!).

You can jump into a drill and be the target for a few minutes (players get a point for passing it into the coach. Make it so it has to hit you below the knees though otherwise balls will be going everywhere)!

Or jump into a game, join one of the teams and say **"I am the best player in the world! No one can beat me!"** and watch the energy level go up from all the players.

7. LEARN ABOUT (AND FROM) YOUR PLAYERS

It's easy to go through a whole season without learning too much about your players or team mates outside of football. Coaching kids soccer keeps you young so make sure to find out what is going on in their world! Ask them about family, school, favourite soccer players, favourite foods, music, what they did on the weekend etc.

I also coach a men's team (mostly 18 to 30 year olds) and in our Facebook group chat, I get them to put a thumbs up or down for who can attend training that week. And along with asking who can attend training I ask them a question for the week as well. For example it might be something as simple as "What did you do on the weekend?".

Or I have asked "What do your parents do for a living?", "What can you cook?", "Tell us your best joke", or "Hardest thing you've had to deal with?".

If it's a fairly personal thing make sure to say "If you feel comfortable sharing something about..." so they don't feel pressured.

And if it's a brand new group I might start it off with answering the question myself to break the ice.

I have found this to be a great experience in bringing the players closer together and they enjoy their time around each other more no matter if they win, lose or draw.

End of Part 3 "FURTHER SOCCER SKILLS" section

SUMMARY

The main focus for most players at this age is to make sure they have fun. If they do, they will keep coming back and will practise and play at home as well. So as a coach if you're making your sessions fun that's half the job done!

So let's finish up with reminding you of a few key things from the start of the book to keep in mind when you take your next training session.

(**Side note:** Thanks for getting my book and supporting me. If you could **spend a minute and review my book on Amazon it would mean a lot as it helps others find it.** Just search "Chris King Soccer" on Amazon, click on the book you bought and if you scroll down you will see a button that says "Write A Customer Review").

Things to keep in mind when coaching young children:

- You will have different levels of skill and experience amongst the children so make sure to **encourage and praise all the players** - not just the ones that are at a better skill level

- Create opportunities where **all the children can experience success**

- **Be patient** and give them time to grasp what you are showing them

- Use games that encourage **every child to have a ball at their feet as much as possible**

- **Praise each child for their effort** no matter what the end result

- **Keep the children excited!** Act crazy or be over enthusiastic if you need to be

- **Use simple language** to explain and make sure to demonstrate as well

- **Encourage players to be creative**

- **Keep it fun** so they will want to come back next time

Thank you and happy coaching!
Chris King

OTHER SOCCER COACHING BOOKS BY CHRIS KING

Other soccer books by Chris King available on Amazon: https://amzn.to/3nmgK6B

Follow Chris at www.facebook.com/chriskingsoccercoach and sign up for free updates/drills/skills at his website www.chriskingsoccercoach.com

"Coaching Kids Soccer Volume 1"

COACHING KIDS SOCCER

AGES 5 TO 10
VOLUME 3

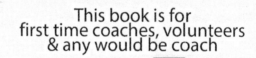

This book is for
first time coaches, volunteers
& any would be coach

Set up simple, fun and effective drills &
organise a practice session in 5 minutes!

CHRIS KING

COACHING KIDS
SOCCER

AGES 5 TO 10 - VOLUME 3

20 FUN SOCCER DRILLS THAT TEACH SOCCER SKILLS TO 5 TO 10 YEAR OLDS PLUS GENERAL COACHING ADVICE

This book is for amateur grassroots coaches, volunteers and parents.

After reading this book you will be able to run a kids soccer training session with confidence!

This book is aimed at coaching 5 to 10 year olds soccer. It has 20 soccer games that will help improve the four main aspects that kids should focus on in their early development:

1. **Passing**
2. **Dribbling**
3. **Shooting**
4. **1v1**

You can choose any of the games from this book to use at training and they will improve at least one (if not all four!) of those skills.

You will also learn how to structure a kids training session using the games from this book that develop soccer skills while at the same time making sure the kids have lots of fun!

So let's jump into it.

HOW TO STRUCTURE A KIDS TRAINING SESSION

Here is how I layout a kids training session.

I would encourage you to structure your training session the same as I have below.

Children like some structure. So if you follow the session layout you will find that children soon get to know what to do as the season progresses, which makes training easier for them and coaching more enjoyable for you.

(Note: If you also coach youth and adult teams, my book "Training Sessions For Soccer Coaches Book 1" lays out how to structure training sessions for youth and adult teams as well as which drills to use).

My training sessions are split into 5 Parts. So whatever amount of time you have, simply divide the time into 5 and spend equal amounts of time on each part. Easy! (Note: Allow 10 minutes for talking and explaining drills throughout the session).

PRE TRAINING: SMALL SIDED GAME	PART 1: ESSENTIAL SKILL PRACTISE	PART 2: FUN GAME	PART 3: SMALL SIDED GAME (with slight change)	PART 4: FUN GAME	PART 5: SMALL SIDED GAME
Kids go straight into a game as they start arriving at training.	Practise a skill that will be the focus of the session. (ie Passing; Dribbling; 1v1; Shooting)	Fun games related to soccer. A chance for kids to spend time on the ball & experience success.	3v3 up to 5v5 on a small pitch with goals. Encourage the main skill that is the focus of the session.	Fun games related to soccer. A chance for kids to spend time on the ball & experience success.	3v3 up to 5v5 on a small pitch with goals.

Okay let's get started by explaining the first section…

PRE-TRAINING: SMALL SIDED GAME - Use this as children arrive at training up until the official training start time.

This is a great way to start the session before it's actually started! As kids turn up, simply get them straight into a game! There might be at least a 15 minute gap between the first child arriving and training actually starting, so why waste this time? Get them into a game and this helps them get extra touches on the ball and improve their soccer skills before training has even started.

As kids turn up, give them a bib and let them loose in a game! Parents can join in to make up the numbers to start with.

1. Have 1 or 2 small fields marked out (approx 20x15 metres). I know you may only have limited space if you are waiting for other teams to finish training but try and find a small area somewhere.

2. Organise the children into 2 teams as they turn up (have two sets of bibs on the ground ready to go). Try to keep it to a maximum of 4 or 5 a side so that all the players are getting plenty of touches. If there are more than 8-10 players, get another game going in the next square.

3. Simply throw a ball in the middle and away they go! Now they are having fun and getting better at soccer before training has even started!

PART 1: ESSENTIAL SKILL PRACTISE - This is the time where we want the children to get lots of touches on the ball and work on their essential/fundamental skills.

Get them all to grab a ball and then show and tell them what skill they will be working on in this training session.

If it's with really young players, it may just be showing them how to do Toe Taps or Sol Rolls. If this is the case, show and tell them how to do it and get them straight into it (they learn by doing)! Then you can go around as they practise and help them out individually.

Stop them after a minute or two and re-show them and get one of the kids to show everyone the skill as well.

If they are older players you may be working on Turns or Passing. If this is the case, in the following Parts (Part 2 through to Part 5) try to make sure to emphasise and encourage Turns or Passing as they play.

PART 2: FUN GAME - A fun game related to soccer. This is a chance for kids to spend time on the ball and experience success.

Use any drill from this book or my previous two (Coaching Kids Soccer Volume 1 and Coaching Kids Soccer Volume 2).

Make sure to put emphasis on one main skill that you are working on in this session (ie Passing; Dribbling; Shooting; 1v1).

PART 3: SMALL SIDED GAME (with a slight change) - Play 3v3 up to 5v5 on a small pitch with goals (any more than 5v5, set up another pitch so players get plenty of touches). During the game make sure to encourage the main skill that is the focus of the session (ie Passing; Dribbling; Shooting; 1v1).

TIP: You can do this by awarding double goals if the skill is performed in the lead up to the goal. **For example, if you are working on passing for this session, make the slight change that if a team makes 5 passes before scoring a goal, they get awarded 2 goals.**

PART 4: FUN GAME - The same as Part 1, this is another fun game related to soccer. This is another chance for kids to spend time playing soccer, improve their skills and experience success.

Use any drill from this book or my previous two (Coaching Kids Soccer Volume 1 and Coaching Kids Soccer Volume 2)

PART 5: SMALL SIDED GAME - Back to playing a game! 3v3 up to 5v5 on a small pitch with goals. Don't make any rule changes here. Simply encourage them to have fun and allow the kids to explore playing against each other. Let them learn by doing!

So that is how to structure your training session. Fairly easy isn't it?

Before getting into the fun soccer games that I've put

together for you, here are a few things to keep in mind when training young children (make sure to reread these points every couple of weeks so they stay front of mind):

- You will have kids with different levels of skill and experience, so make sure to **encourage and praise all the players** - not just the ones that are at a better skill level. They all develop at a different rate.

- Create opportunities where **all the children can experience success (ie a drill where everyone gets to score a goal or work on a skill and improve it).**

- **Be patient** and give them time to grasp what you are showing them (make sure to demonstrate skills - kids pick things up easier by observing than just listening to an explanation).

- Use games that encourage **every child to have a ball at their feet as much as possible.**

- **Praise each child for their effort,** no matter what the end result.

- **Keep the children excited!** Act like a clown or be over enthusiastic if you need to be.

- **Use simple language** to explain things and make sure to demonstrate the skill or drill.

- **Encourage players to be creative.**

- **Keep it fun** so they will want to come back next time.

PRE-PRACTICE TIPS FOR THE COACH
- Arrive early so your games/areas are set up.

- As mentioned in the Training Session Structure,

when the children start arriving, organise them into a game straight away.

- Enjoy the session! Forget about anything else that is happening in your life and just enjoy coaching the children.

EQUIPMENT NEEDED (IF POSSIBLE)
- 1 ball per child
- 12 cones
- 2 or 4 mini goals (use poles or cones if no goals)
- 4 sets of different coloured bibs

SETTING UP
If you're not sure exactly how many children you will have for the session, it's best to set up an extra 'mirror drill' (two of the same drill) just in case.

I like to set the two areas up side by side with a channel in the middle where I can see both areas and therefore keep an eye on everything. Plus I can distribute balls to both areas.

Tip: *You can lose children's attention very quickly, so by having everything set up as much as possible ahead of time and therefore not having to stop to set up during a session, it leads to the kids not getting distracted and a smoothly run session.*

Use the same coloured cones for one pitch and a different set of coloured cones for the other. This is so it is clear to the children which pitch is which. (Then, for example, you can say to them "Team 1 and 2 on the pitch with yellow cones" and they know where to go straight away).

See the images below for how I set up (this example has 12

children with two 3v3 games) and then we'll get into the fun soccer games!

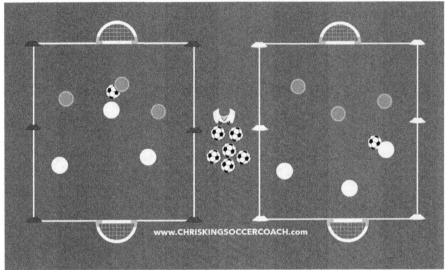

This is how I set up my games and position myself if I have two small areas. I can keep an eye on both and distribute balls to both pitches.

Happy Coaching!
Chris King

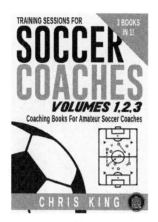

20 FUN SOCCER DRILLS

GAME #1
"POLES"

□ FOCUS OF SESSION:

This is a simple but effective drill. "Poles" help kids with their dribbling skills, getting their head up to scan the area, changing direction with the ball and keeping close possession.

□ SET UP:

- **4 to 12 players**
- 25x25 yard square
- 6 Poles

□ THE DRILL:

In a large square, randomly spread poles around the area. Players start inside the square with a ball each.

They must dribble around as many poles as they can in a set amount of time (usually 1 minute), avoiding other players.

After 1 minute, call out "Stop" and all players should be able to put their foot on the ball. If the ball is too far away and they can't stop it straight away, this means the player hasn't kept close control. Give those players a small task to do (5 toe taps on the ball) to encourage them to keep close control next time.

Ask how many poles each player got around in the minute. Then see if they can improve on their next round.

Call out different parts of the foot to use (ie "Soles only!" "Outside of the foot only" "Right foot only!). This all helps their development and confidence.

COACHES NOTES:

- Players should have close control so that in a game defenders can't steal the ball from them. Every now and then, walk around the square and lightly kick the kids' balls if the ball is too far from their body. This shows them how a Defender could steal it.

- Players should be regularly looking around so they can see where the next pole is and so they can avoid the other players.

☑ CHANGE IT:

Encourage personal improvement - for example, can they get around 6 poles in 1 minute the first go? Then the next minute can they beat their last attempt and get around 8?

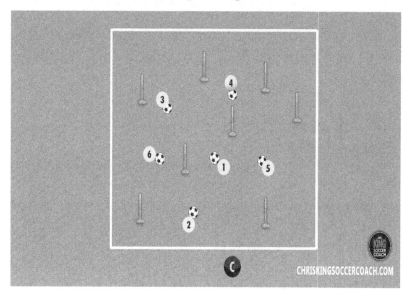

CHRISKINGSOCCERCOACH.COM

Each player starts with a ball. When the coach calls out "Go!" players try to get around as many poles as they can.

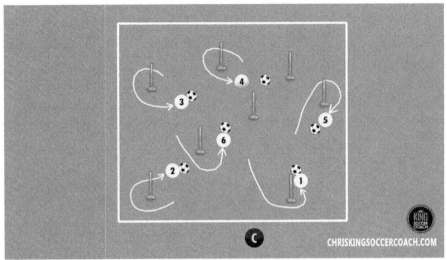

Players must keep close control and get their heads up so they don't run into other players or balls. In the above image, #4's ball is a bit too far from them and the ball could be stolen in a game situation.

GAME #2
"MOST BALLS WINS"

☐ FOCUS OF SESSION:

Dribbling and ball control in a game situation. Winning back possession.

☐ SET UP:

- **8 to 12 players**
  8 players use 4 teams of 2
  9 players use 4 teams (3 teams with 2 players and 1 team with 3)
  10 players use 4 teams (2 teams with 3 players and 2 teams with 2)
  11 players use 4 teams (3 teams with 3 players and 1 team with 2)
  12 players use 4 teams with 3 players.

- 25x25 yard square
- 4 smaller squares in the corners of the large square
- Lots of balls ready to be kicked or thrown in!

☐ THE DRILL:

Players are split into 4 teams and aim to dribble and leave as many balls in their team's small square as possible.

All players start near their small square. The coach throws balls into the centre at random times (feel free to throw a couple at once).

Players run in and compete to try to win possession of a ball and dribble it back and stop it in their square.

Other players without a ball can tackle a player and try to win possession.

Once all the balls are in the small squares, count up who has the most and that team wins!

☐ COACHES NOTES:

- Having the players stop the ball in the square helps with their close control. Players shouldn't be just kicking and chasing the ball with the balls going way past their square. Make sure to give a demonstration before starting on how close control dribbling looks and how to stop the ball. (Lots of little touches with the feet so the ball isn't too far ahead and stop it with the sole of the foot).

- Make sure to throw and roll the balls in at different speeds and heights so players are practising different control techniques.

- Try and get the players to concentrate. If they don't have a ball make sure they are looking around to either try and win possession off an opponent or they are ready for when the coach throws a new ball in.

☑ CHANGE IT:

#1 - Join two teams together so, for example, there would be 4v4 in an 8 player game.

#2 - Use different skills while dribbling - i.e. players must use just their left foot or players must perform a sole roll while dribbling back.

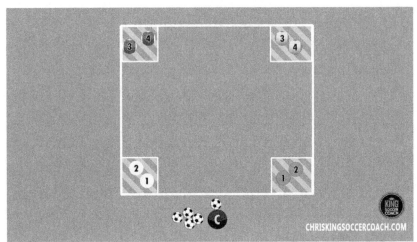

Players start in their small squares with the coach ready to throw some balls in.

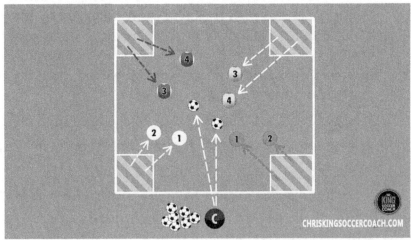

As soon as the balls are kicked/thrown in, players can run in and compete to win the ball.

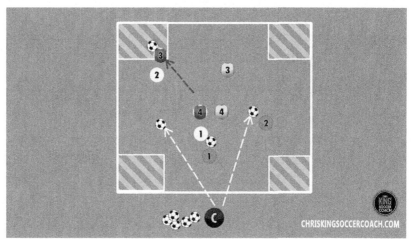

Here Dark #3 has won a ball and dribbled it back to their square and stopped it. Light #1 and Darkish #1 are competing for a ball.
Play until all balls have been dribbled into a small square and count up how many each team has. The most balls win.

GAME #3
"SANTA/PARTY HATS"

☐ **FOCUS OF SESSION:**

Getting the players to have fun while getting used to a game situation. Players will use all four main skills: Dribbling, Passing, 1v1, Shooting.

Note: **This drill can be adjusted for anytime of the year**, not just Christmas! Simply swap the Santa hats for party hats, pirate hats, regular caps (get the kids to bring their own!) etc.

☐ **SET UP:**
- **4 to 12 players**
  (either 2v2, 3v3, 4v4, 5v5 or 6v6)
- Small 20x15 yard pitch with small goals at each end
- Split the players into two teams
- Have Santa hats ready for players to put on

⬜ THE DRILL:

Simple! Regular soccer rules but each time a team scores, one player gets to put a Santa hat on.

Once every player on a team has a Santa hat on that team wins!

⬜ COACHES NOTES:

- A game situation like this uses all aspects of soccer - communication, movement, plus all different skills (passing, dribbling, taking players on 1v1, shooting). So players will naturally be working on different skills.

  But every now and then bring in a restriction for two minutes to help them focus on one particular skill.

  For example, make restrictions such as:
  1. There must be three passes before a goal can be scored.
  2. A player must dribble past an opponent before a goal can be scored.
  3. All players must touch the ball before a goal can be scored.

This helps to work on different skills but also helps them to communicate and concentrate on the task at hand.

☑ CHANGE IT:

#1 - If a player can name three of Santa's reindeers they get an extra Santa hat.

#2 - If a player can spell "reindeer or Christmas" they get an extra hat.

#3 - I think you can see where this is going. See if you can come up with some other fun, Christmasy ones.

Ho! Ho! Ho!

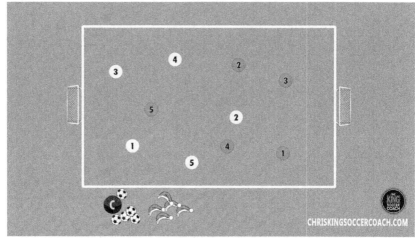

Players are ready for action. Who can be the first team to score 5 goals and get a Santa hat for every player?

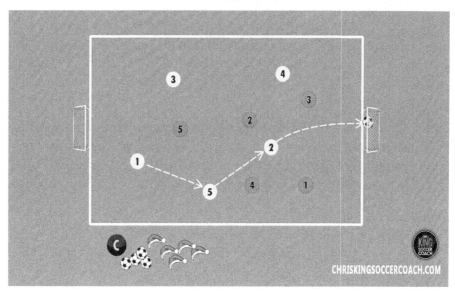

The Light team passes the ball well and scores a goal so they get a Santa hat.

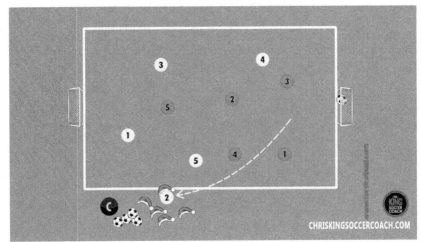

Light #2 puts it on and everyone keeps playing until one team has all their players in a Santa hat.

GAME #4
"BIBS"

☐ **FOCUS OF SESSION:**
This drill helps with young players' basic and fundamental movement skills. At an early age, players are still learning what their bodies can do. So in this drill they will get to develop speed, change of direction and spatial awareness.

☐ **SET UP:**
- **5 to 16 players**
- 25 yard circle
- A bib for every player

☐ **THE DRILL:**
Sometimes called "Tails", "Bibs" simply involves each player tucking a bib into the back of their shorts (so it looks like they have a tail).

Note: Make sure that half the bib is in and half is out otherwise you will get some players tucking 95% of it in their shorts so other players can't get it!

Before starting the actual game, get all players to start by moving around the circle, dodging this way and that, turning and moving in all directions. They are just getting used to avoiding each other, faking out each other, quick changes of direction etc. At this stage you can call out a few instructions if you wish (i.e. faster, left, backwards, etc), otherwise just let them run and move.

Once the coach shouts "Go!' all the players must try and steal each other's bibs out from the back of their shorts. Their aim is to try and win as many as possible (they hold the bibs they win in their hands)!

After 1 minute (or once everyone has had their bib stolen), shout "Stop!" and players count up how many bibs they grabbed. The player with the most gets a high five from the coach! ☐ Or they get to shout "I am the best Bib player in the world!!!" (Similar to Billy Madison in his spelling bee contest).

☐ COACHES NOTES:

- **Changes of speed!** I can't mention this enough. A quick burst of speed can soon get a player out of trouble. Teach the players to get in the habit of exploding away when they decide to change directions.

- **Faking!** Teach the players to do an exaggerated step one way (which will unbalance a defender in a game) and then go the other way. The same with a shoulder drop - get the players to drop their shoulder as if they were going one way and then get them to move off in the opposite direction.

  Note: In a game situation, a good deceptive tactic is raising an arm as if you are getting ready to shoot. The defender sees this and subconsciously puts out their leg to block the shot/long pass or they stop to put their body or leg in the way. When this happens the Attacker can go past them.

- **Look around!** Teach the players to get their heads up whenever they can. This will feel unnatural in their early development when they are still learning skills. But it will become easier as they get more familiar with the ball. Looking around helps with knowing where to pass, what spaces to move/dribble into and where the opposition and teammates are.

☑ CHANGE IT:

#1 - Players dribble a ball as they try to steal bibs!

#2 - Split the players into teams and players work as a team to try to get all the other teams bibs. First team to get all the other teams' bibs wins!

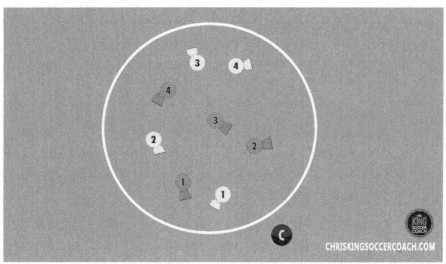

All players start with a bib tucked into the back of their shorts. Play until all the bibs have been taken and then count up who got the most.

GAME #5
"BANK ROBBERS"

☐ FOCUS OF SESSION:

Dribbling, passing and evasive skills.

⬜ SET UP:

- **6 to 18 players**
- 30x20 yard rectangle with 2 small squares off to either side
- 2 bibs
- Lots of balls

⬜ THE DRILL:

This drill is lots of fun! Two police (in bibs) against a whole lot of little bank robbers trying to steal soccer balls from the bank vault!

Set up a large rectangle with a zone at the end. This zone is used as a bank and has all the balls spread out in it.

Set up two small squares off to either side of the rectangle (use cones or poles) - this is the jail where players go if they get caught (tagged) by the police with a stolen ball.

Note: *You decide if the police simply tag the robbers or if they have to kick their ball out for the robbers to be caught on their way back.*

Choose two players to be the police and they start in the middle of the rectangle with bibs on.

Get the other players to pair up and they start at the opposite end to the bank.

One player from each pair races into the middle and tries to make it to the bank without getting caught (tagged) by the police! If they get caught they run back to their partner and let them have a turn at robbing the bank.

If they are successful at getting to the bank, they get a ball and try to get it back to their partner without getting tagged. They can either dribble or pass it back to their partner.

But if they get caught (tagged) by the police on their way back they have to return their ball to the bank, go to jail (either of the two small squares to the side) and do 5 jumping jacks. Their partner can go while they are in jail.

As soon as all the balls have been successfully stolen from the bank, count up the balls to see which pair has the most money (each ball is worth 1 000 000 pounds!).

☐ COACHES NOTES:

- To avoid being caught by the police, are the players using: Change of speed? Quick change of direction? Body feints (dropping the shoulder or stepping one way and going the other)? All this helps in their development of body movement.

- Are the players using both dribbling and passing to get the ball back to their partner? There is no right or wrong here. As long as they are trying both they will improve their decision making on when to dribble past an opponent and when to pass. If there is an obvious, easy pass back to their partner, they should get in the habit of passing. As my old coach used to say, "It's quicker to pass a ball to your teammate than to dribble it to them".

- Are the police (the Defenders) shepherding a robber towards one side so they don't have as many options to get past them? Also, the Defenders shouldn't rush in full steam because the robbers can then just pick a side and go past. Instead they should jockey a little bit and pick their moment to tag the robber.

☑ CHANGE IT:

#1 - Add more police or remove a police officer depending on numbers or skill levels of the players. Or make the Coach the police officer! I often like to make myself the Defender in a drill and that way I can coach and encourage the kids while I'm out amongst them.

#2 - Give the players bibs to tuck into their shorts and the police have to grab the bib for the robber to be caught! And make it so if the police grab 5 bibs they win and every robber has to do 10 jumping jacks.

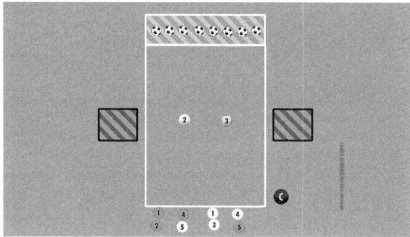

Two police start in the middle (White #2 and #3). The bank robbers start at the bottom, ready to try and get past the police and steal a ball from the bank!

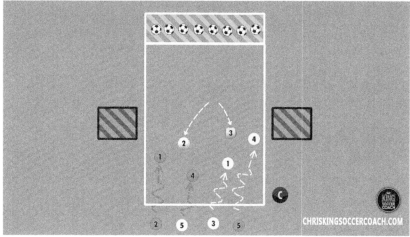

The first player from the pair all run out, dodging and weaving to try and get past the police.

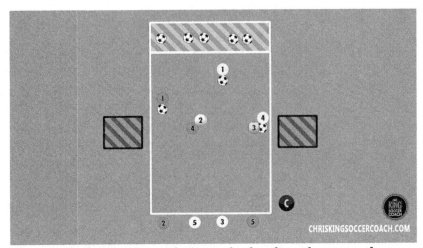

Dark and Light #1's made it to the bank and are on the way back to their partner. Dark #4 got caught by the Police (#2) and must return and let their partner have a try. Light #4 got caught with a ball so must return it to the bank vault and go to jail and perform 5 jumping jacks.

INTERMISSION

Now is a good time to explain three of the basic skills that kids will be using in the next drill. Toe Taps, Sole Rolls and Happy Feet are all footwork skills that help build a young players' touch on the ball.

Also, a bit of "beginner juggling" helps with controlling the ball at different heights and with different parts of the body.

TOE TAPS

Toe Taps are simply touches on the top of the ball using the sole of the shoe. They help improve coordination, improve players quickness of feet and improve their touch on the ball.

How to do Toe Taps:

The player should stand with the ball directly in front of them.

They then put the sole of one foot on top of the ball while keeping the other one planted on the ground.

Then switch feet so the opposite sole of the foot is on the ball and the other foot is on the ground. Repeat this. (it's similar to marching on the spot except you place the sole of the foot on the ball each time).

Players should go as slowly as required to start with. Eventually they will be doing it in a fluid motion. Build up so that eventually players will be "bouncing" as they do it (moving one foot as soon as the other touches the top of the ball).

TOE TAPS

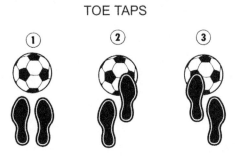

SOLE ROLLS

This helps with a players' touch and learning to move the ball.

How to do Sole Rolls:
Simply roll the ball softly *with the sole of the foot* in any direction. Then, with the same foot, roll it back to the starting position. For example, roll it out to the right with the sole of the right foot, then roll it back to the starting position with the sole of the right foot.

Start by doing it in the one spot and then progress to moving around the ground doing it.

Once they have the hang of it, players can roll it forward, backwards or whichever direction they want with the sole of either foot.

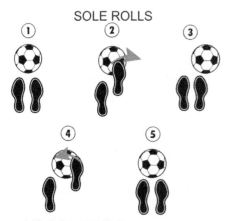

HAPPY FEET

Happy Feet are when the player is tapping the ball back and forth between the instep of their feet. Use the instep of both feet and tap it back and forth. Think of it like that old computer game "Pong".

This helps with players' touch on the ball, coordination and quick feet.

How To Do Happy Feet:
1. Start slow jogging on the spot
2. Step up to the ball and have it between the feet
3. While still slowly jogging on the spot, lightly tap the ball with the inside of your feet so the ball goes from the left foot to the right foot and back again, continuously.

Tips: Keep the head over the ball, be light on the feet and as always, start slowly until the player gets used to it.

HAPPY FEET
use the inner part of both feet to tap the ball back and forth

Think of it like the old computer game pong. This skill really helps with touch and coordination

BOUNCE JUGGLING (for beginners)

Kids don't want to become frustrated when first learning anything, so bounce juggling is a great way for players to get used to juggling without feeling like it's too hard.

It's simply allowing the ball to bounce in between every juggle (every touch) which allows them to position their body ready for the next juggle without feeling rushed.

HOW TO BOUNCE JUGGLE

1. Pick up the ball using the hands and gently throw it in the air at chest height, slightly out from the body.
2. Let the ball bounce and start to get the body in position and the foot ready to take a juggle touch.
3. Once the ball starts moving down and gets to about knee/shin height, take a touch using the top of the boot.
4. Try to kick the ball to chest/head height. This will allow enough time to get ready for the next touch (as they progress and improve they should aim to mostly kick the ball lower to the

ground).

5. Get balanced so they are ready for the next touch. Let the ball bounce and then repeat!

6. Make sure to use both feet and progress to using thighs, chest and head once used to juggling with just the feet.

OK, let's get back into the games!

GAME #6
"BALL CONTROL"

▢ **FOCUS OF SESSION:**
Improve the players' ball control so they are more confident on the ball and in 1v1 situations.

▢ **SET UP:**
- **6 to 9 players**
  (for more than 6 players adjust the size of the circle accordingly)
- Large circle
- 2 to 3 goals spread evenly around the outside of the circle (2 goals for 6 players. 3 goals for 7 to 9 players)

▢ **THE DRILL:**
Players are dribbling around the circle working on their ball control (aka ball manipulation).

Firstly they use different parts of their feet: Dribbling with the insteps, dribbling with the outside of the feet, sole rolls, happy feet, toe taps, turns, etc. The coach should be calling out which skill to use.

Secondly, move onto juggling. Get the players to count how many juggles they can do and then see if they can beat their highest score. Even if it's only 1 or 2 juggles, this helps with the players being able to control the soccer ball at different heights and eventually with different parts of the body.

(<u>Note:</u> View my Coaching Kids Soccer Volume 2 book for more detailed tips on teaching young kids the art of juggling and other kids skills such as dribbling, turns, sole rolls, etc).

Thirdly, call out "Stop". Players put their foot on the ball to stop it and go and find a different ball. This helps with instant control plus it makes sure that the ball is close to them and they aren't just kicking and chasing the ball instead of dribbling.

<u>Note</u>: If you want, make it so the last player to stop their ball has to do 5 toe taps when they get to their new ball. Once you bring this rule in, watch as the players magically keep their ball closer than previously. Plus they will keenly listen out for your instruction to stop so as they're not the last!

Fourthly, remove half the balls and get the players to practise 1v1's in the circle. Have one player defending and the other practising shielding the ball and facing the opponent and try to get past them. Go for 45 seconds and then swap roles.

Lastly, once the players are comfortable with using different skills, juggling, stopping the ball and 1v1 situations, move onto a game within the circle where they can practise all of these skills.

Simply split the players into 2 (or 3) teams (3v3, 4v4, 4v4+1 Joker, 3v3v3 [use 3 goals]) and play a game!

☐ COACHES NOTES:

- Make sure players use all parts of their feet to dribble, turn and shield the ball (inside and outside of both feet, sole rolls, etc).

- When players shield the ball, make sure to get them to use their furthest foot from the defender to control the ball. This way they have the ball under control but also it is out of reach of the defender.

- Also, when shielding the ball, can they keep their elbows

up to the side of their body to make themselves bigger? I like to call this chicken wings. Call it this and the kids will remember it. And next time you say "Don't forget about your chicken wings!" watch them put their arms/elbows up beside their body to make themselves bigger and protect/shield the ball.

- Get the players to keep their head up when possible. This helps in seeing where they can pass a ball or run into space and also where the defender is coming from.

- Encourage players to take their defender on, especially if they are facing them.

- **This drill is great for the kids' confidence with ball control. They firstly get to practise the skills unopposed, then 1v1 and later on in a game situation.**

☑ CHANGE IT:

Put the coach or a parent in the circle and try to steal the players' balls. Make it exciting! Say things like "Right! Here comes the coach! I'm going to win the ball off Michael and Ingrid!" and watch those players smile, laugh and try even harder!

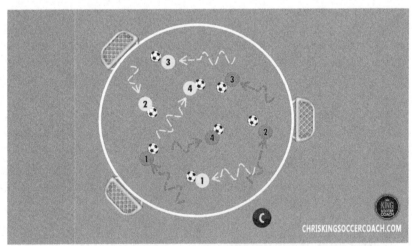

Firstly players dribble around the circle using different parts of their feet and performing different skills (insteps, sole rolls, happy feet, toe taps, turns, etc).

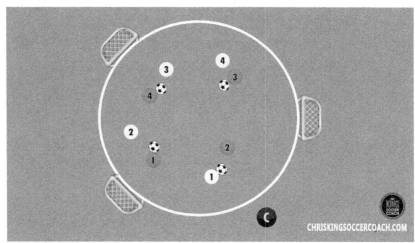

After practising a bit of juggling and stopping and swapping balls, players move on to 1v1's. Remove half the balls and get the players to practise 1v1's in the circle.

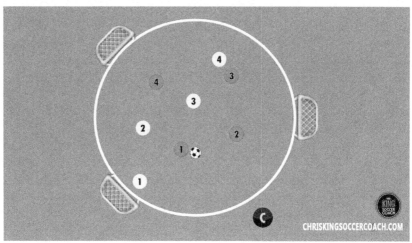

Lastly, split the players into two teams and play a game where they can use all the skills they've just been practising. They can score in any goal.

GAME #7
"OUCH"

⬜ **FOCUS OF SESSION:**

To encourage the kids to get their heads up while they dribble. This helps them to become aware of where the options are to pass and where the Defenders are.

This drill also helps with striking at a target.

⬜ **SET UP:**
- **5 to 12 players + at least 1 Coach (or parent)!**
- 20x20 yard square

⬜ **THE DRILL:**

What more can a player ask for than to get to kick a ball at the coach? In this game that's exactly what they get to do!

Each player starts inside the square with a ball and the coach starts inside the square without a ball.

When the coach says "Go!" players get to kick the ball at the coach - *aiming for below the knees!* This drill helps with the players being able to strike a ball on the move and also with scanning the area.

Each time the coach gets hit they should yell out "Ouch!" or something silly.

Play for 2 minutes, get the kids to keep count of how many times they have hit the coach and the player that has kicked their ball into the coach the most gets a high five from all the players.

⬜ **COACHES NOTES:**
- Make sure to say that it has to be below the knee for it to count.

- The coach should change directions, dodge and weave so that the players have to look up to see where they are.

- Show the players the correct technique for passing/ striking a ball: Eyes up to look at the target and then eyes back down on the ball to strike it. If it's a close range shot, it can be a pass with the instep. But if it's longer range, show them how to shoot with the laces to get more power.

☑ CHANGE IT:

#1 - If the kids are struggling to hit the coach, slow down and stay in one spot for a second or two to make it easier for them.

#2 - Can players use both feet to dribble and shoot?

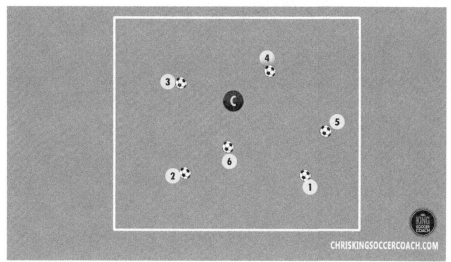

All the players start inside the square with a ball each. Once the coach says "Go!" the coach starts dodging around the square and the players get to pass/strike the ball into the coach (below the knee!).

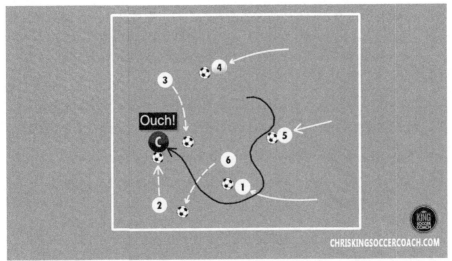

#6 and #3 missed the coach but #2's was a good strike and hit the coach below the knee!

GAME #8
"1v1"

☐ FOCUS OF SESSION:
Good ball control so as to be able to beat an opponent 1v1.

☐ SET UP:
- **6 to 10 players**
- 35x30 yard rectangle
- 6 mini goals

☐ THE DRILL:
Set up a large rectangle (approx 35x30 yards). Place 3 mini goals at each end.

Pair the players up, start at opposite ends with one player with a ball.

The Defender passes the ball to the Attacker who takes control and tries to beat the Defender and score in the goal closest to them at the other end.

If the Defender wins the ball they can try and score in the goal at the opposite end.

Swap roles after each turn.

Note: *Make sure to limit each go to approximately 10-20 seconds. We want to encourage the players to go at the Defender, as opposed to stopping, going back, shielding the ball, etc.*

☐ **COACHES NOTES:**

- Make sure the players keep close control. They may want to dribble too fast but they need to keep it under control, otherwise it is easy for the Defender to win the ball. If they have lots of space in front of them they can take longer strides/touches (i.e. have more than 1 step in between each touch). But when the Defender is closer they should be shorter touches (one step for every touch) so they can change direction easily and keep it away from the Defender.

- The Attacker should get their heads up as much as possible so they are away of where the Defender is. They should use different parts of the foot to change direction and get past the Defender.

- Different speeds can also help in getting past opponents. If they send the Defender one way with a feint, can they speed off the other direction?

☑ **CHANGE IT:**

- Team players up and play 2v2.

- Team all the players up into two teams and play against each other.

- If you don't have enough space or players are getting tired, have 2 pairs behind each other and take it in turns.

- Set up a cone for the players to practise against before moving on to a real 1v1 situation.

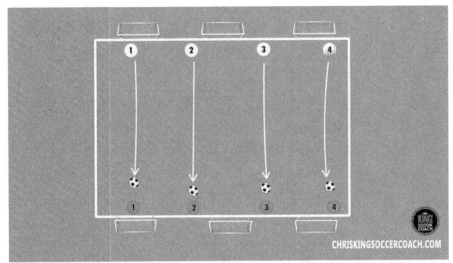

Players get to practise 1v1 situations. Defenders (Light) start with the ball and pass the ball to the Attackers (Dark) to start play.

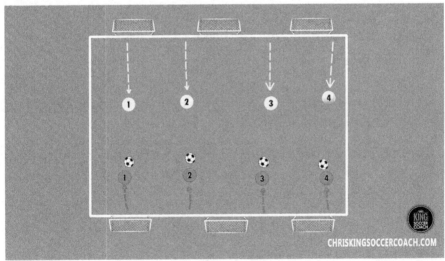

Defenders get out to the Attackers as fast as they can to shut them down. Attackers get to practise feints, shoulders drops, going at pace, etc to get past their Defender and score in the goal. Swap after each go.

GAME #9

"4 GOAL FUN SOCCER"

☐ FOCUS OF SESSION:

Let the kids learn by playing - just play soccer and have fun like they would at lunchtime at school. All skills will be worked on naturally.

☐ SET UP:

- **6 to 12 players**
- 35x25 yard rectangle
- 4 mini goals

☐ THE DRILL:

We want the kids to learn by doing, have success (i.e. score goals!) and not worry about any consequences of making mistakes. So let them play soccer and score lots of goals!

Set up a 35x25 yard rectangle with 4 goals (one on each side).

Split the players into 4 teams (ie if 8 players have 4 teams of 2. If you only have 6 players, have 3 teams of 2).

All teams play at once and can score in any goal!

As soon as a ball goes out or a goal is scored the coach should put another one in straight away. Also, sometimes put two balls at once! Twice the chaos, twice the fun and twice the goals.

The first team to 5 goals wins, then swap teams around.

☐ COACHES NOTES:

- Make sure everyone is having fun! Lots of encouragement and celebrating when goals are scored (high fives, rolly pollies, etc!).

- Encourage players to dribble, pass, take players on and shoot. This is a great chance for them to work out how to do things in a game situation.

☑ CHANGE IT:

#1 - Combine two teams (ie 4v4.). No need to even stop the game, just call out "Blues and greens are together versus yellow and reds."

#2 - Play 3 teams v 1. And if it's too hard for the 1 team, maybe the coach can join in and help them?

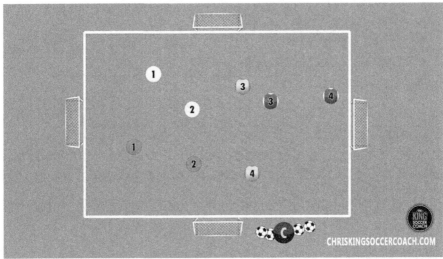

4 teams with 2 players each - players can score in any goal. This drill is all about having fun and scoring goals. Players get to practise all the skills they are learning (dribbling, passing, taking players on and shooting) in a fun environment.

GAME #10
"SURFERS AND SHARKS"

☐ **FOCUS OF SESSION:**

Dribbling and tackling (and passing when using the progression change).

☐ **SET UP:**

- **8 to 18 players**
- 35x25 rectangle with 3 different sized small squares inside the area

⬜ THE DRILL:

Choose two players to be sharks who wait in the rectangle. The rest of the players are surfers who each have a ball and start at one end.

Players practise their dribbling skills, aiming to surf (dribble) from one end of the ocean to the other without getting eaten (tackled) by a shark.

If a shark tackles a surfer and wins the ball or kicks it out they swap roles.

If the surfers need to, they can have a quick rest on one of the islands which are safe zones.

Once surfers reach the other end they turn around and come back. Who can get to the most ends? Get the players to count as they go!

Note: *Add or remove sharks if it's too easy or too hard for the surfers.*

⬜ COACHES NOTES:

- Encourage players to use different parts of their feet when dribbling (inside and outside of both feet and soles).

- Use a change of speed (or direction!) to get past the sharks.

- Stop the ball on the islands (this will mean that players should have close control so they can stop it when required).

- Shield the ball when required. Can they keep the ball on the other side of the body so the shark can't tackle and steal the ball from them? Players should keep their arms/elbows up to help make them bigger and keep the sharks away from the ball.

- Sharks should look to win possession as soon as they can. If they've just become a shark, encourage them to keep their head up and win a ball back straight away. This helps in a real game situation as they won't give up if they lose a ball. They will get in the habit of trying to win back possession for their team straight away.

- Make sure surfers aren't spending too long on the islands. If they do, bring in a 5-10 second limit.

☑ CHANGE IT:

#1 - Add players (or parents) to the side and the surfers can do a one two pass with them to avoid being caught with the ball.

#2 - Add goals at each end. If surfers successfully make it from one end to the other they can have a shot at goal and receive a bonus point. Play for 5 minutes and see who gets the most points.

#3 - Team players up and give a ball to each pair and see if they can pass their way through the ocean without being eaten by the sharks!

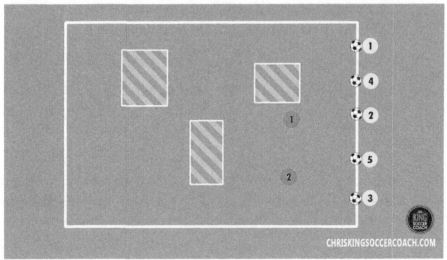

The two sharks (Dark #1 and 2) wait in the middle to see if they can catch a surfer and win the ball off them!

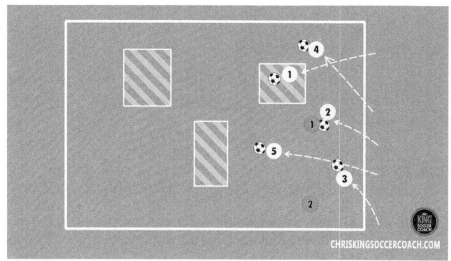

Light #4 is smart and goes wide away from the sharks. Light #1 goes straight for the first island, is safe and can plan their next move. Light #2 gets eaten (tackled and loses the ball) by a shark and must swap roles and become the shark.

GAME #11
"HIT THE CONE"

□ FOCUS OF SESSION:

Defensive skills and accurate passing. Kids love this simple soccer drill!

□ SET UP:

- **4 to 16 players**
- 10x10 yard square

□ THE DRILL:

Set up a 10x10 yard square with a tall cone in the middle (or a regular cone with a ball on top).

4 players per square with 1 player defending the cone and the other 3 passing the ball around the square and trying to knock the cone over by passing the ball into it.

The Defender must block any passes and kick the balls away to stop the attack on their cone!

Each round goes for one minute then swap the Defender. The Defender that has their cone knocked over the _least_ amount of times wins.

 COACHES NOTES:
- If you find the Defender is standing right next to the cone, make it so they have to be 3 yards away from the cone.

- Make sure players are moving around the square to receive passes which will make space to have a shot at the cone.

- Players should have their heads up and be scanning the area so they know when to pass, shoot or where to move to.

- Defenders should be on their toes and ready to move, adjust and react as the ball moves.

☑ CHANGE IT:
#1 - Attackers aim to knock the cone over 3 times. Then swap the Defender. Time the Defender to see how long they can defend until their cone is knocked over. Or get the defender to recite the alphabet as many times as they can as they defend the cone. How many times can they get through the alphabet before having their cone knocked over 3 times? The most alphabets wins!

#2 - Require the Attackers to make 3 passes before they can shoot at the cone.

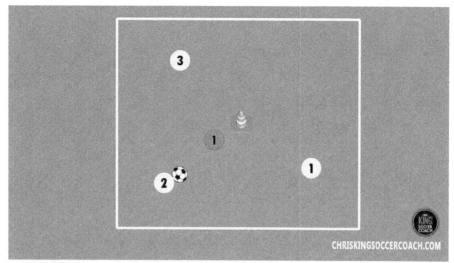

3v1 with the 1 defending the cone and the 3 aiming to pass the ball into the cone to knock it over. Play for 1 minute then swap the Defender.

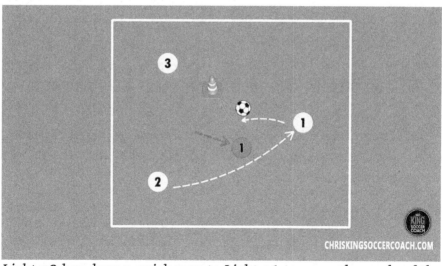

Light #2 has done a quick pass to Light #1 to move the angle of the attack. Dark #1 can't quit cut off the pass and Light #2 is able to knock the cone over.

GAME #12
"PIRATES AND SAILORS"

⬚ FOCUS OF SESSION:

Dribbling in congested areas plus tackling.

⬚ SET UP:

- **6 to 18 players**
- 30 yard circle
- 2 mini goals

⬚ THE DRILL:

Set up a 30 yard circle with 2 mini goals back to back in the middle.

If there are 8 players, have 6 players (Sailors) dribbling a ball around the circle and have 2 players without balls as the Pirates.

The 2 Pirates try to steal the ball off the Sailors and score in either of the mini goals. If they score they swap roles.

(Note: Alternatively play it like British Bulldog rules - if a player loses the ball and the Pirate scores, they become a Pirate and join the other Pirates and play until there is only one Sailor left dribbling with a ball versus all the Pirates!).

⬚ COACHES NOTES:

- The main focus should be on dribbling in traffic. There are lots of moving players and balls. So make sure the Sailors are keeping close control while at the same time scanning the area so they don't run into other players and can see where the Pirates are.

- Pirates should stay focussed once they win the ball so they can score a goal.

☑ CHANGE IT:

#1 - If it's too easy for the Pirates, make the area bigger or have fewer Pirates. Or if it's too hard for the Pirates, let the coach join in to help the Pirates.

#2 - Keep the Pirates in for a set amount of time (ie 2 minutes) and see how many goals they can score. See who can get the most goals after all the players have had a turn at being Pirates.

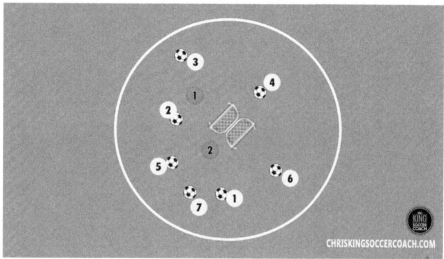

2 Pirates (Red) try to win the ball off the Sailors (Light) and score in one of the mini goals.

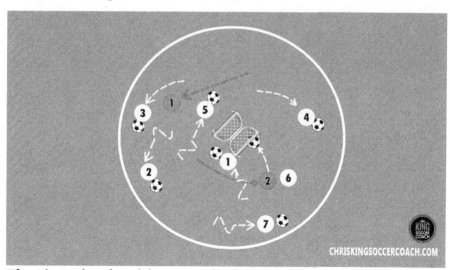

The Pirate (Dark #2) has won the ball off the Sailor (Light #6) and scored so they swap roles.

GAME #13
"1v1 PASSING GAME"

⬜ FOCUS OF SESSION:

Accurate passing and reading the opposition's intentions.

⬜ SET UP:

- **2 players**
- 15x15 yard square

⬜ THE DRILL:

Set up a 15x15 yard square with a 5 yard zone in the middle.

2 players. 1 player starts in each square. Players must pass the ball back and forth to their opponents square and **the ball must either pass through or bounce in the middle zone.**

The aim is to pass a ball so that the opponent can't return it.

Players must play the ball while they are inside their square.

The amount of touches depends on the skill level. Usually 3 touches is about right for 5 to 7 year olds. If players are more skilled, allow less touches. If they are less skilled, allow more touches.

The ball cannot stop dead, so players must use their touches to either pass back first time or make a touch to set up their next pass.

Players receive 1 point if they make a pass to the other square that their opponent can't return. First to 5 points wins the set (play best of 3 sets).

⬜ COACHES NOTES:
- Unless the players are older and more skilled, encourage ground passing.

- Encourage players to pass away from where their opponent is. Or if their opponent is at the front of their square, pass it harder so they can't control it.

- Encourage the players to read their opponents intentions. Are they looking where they are about to pass the ball? Are their hips open and showing which direction they're about to pass? If players can work on reading the opposition's intentions they will become better defenders.

☑ CHANGE IT:

#1 - Use just the weaker foot (this helps improve their weaker foot which pays off as they get older). Refer to it as their "other" or "non-preferred" foot.

#2 - Increase/decrease the number of touches allowed.

#3 - Players can return the pass from outside their square.

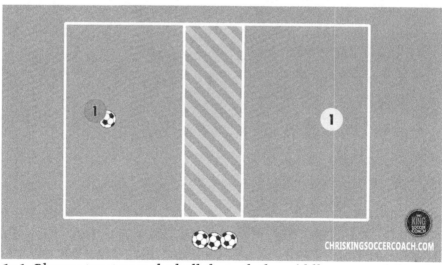

1v1. Players must pass the ball through the middle zone and the aim is for their opponent to not be able to return the pass.

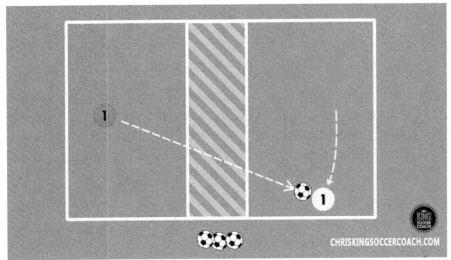

Light has read the pass and gets over to the ball. They must play it while inside the square.

GAME #14
"SOCCER GOLF"

◻ **FOCUS OF SESSION:**

Accurate passing and fun!

◻ **SET UP:**

- **2 to 20 players!**

◻ **THE DRILL:**

Each player has a ball. Play in groups of 2 or 3's.

Pick a target for each group (a goal post, a pole, a garbage bin, a tree, another soccer ball, etc). Players take it in turns of passing their balls to see who can hit the target in the least amount of passes.

For young kids, start each pass with the ball stationary. But for older or more skilled players can they do a skill before the pass? For example, can they do a sole roll (roll the ball with the sole of their foot) or a turn and then pass the ball?

Also, set up poles or other obstacles that the players must pass around or through before aiming for their final target. This will help them improve the weighting of their passes.

☐ COACHES NOTES:

- Encourage players to "weigh" their passes nicely. Say to them "Do you think you'll need a small, medium or big pass for this one?". This will help get it clear in their head how much oomph to put into their passes.

☑ CHANGE IT:

#1 - Alternate feet with every pass (i.e. right foot for the first pass, left foot for the second pass).

#2 - Team up and pass on the move! Play 2v2 and players have to pass their way to the obstacle in the least amount of passes. This will help with teamwork and passing on the move.

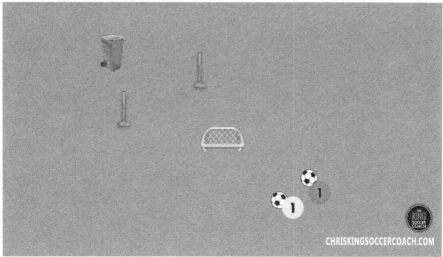

In this example the 2 players must hit the bin. They can choose which way to go around the mini goal and poles.

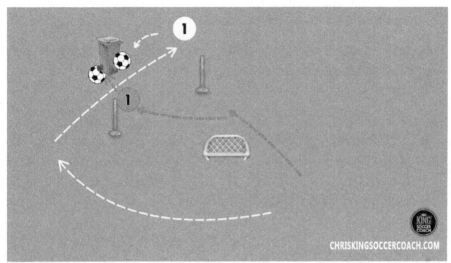

Light went left and it took them 3 passes to hit the bin. Dark went through the middle and also took 3 passes. It's a draw! 1 point each.

GAME #15
"FILL UP THE SQUARE"

☐ FOCUS OF SESSION:

Dribbling and stopping the ball. This drill adds competitiveness and excitement to the session.

☐ SET UP:

- **6 to 20 players**
- 40x30 yard rectangle

☐ THE DRILL:

Set up a 40x30 yard square with two small 5x5 squares in the middle.

Kids (and adults) love relay races! Split the players into two teams, half starting at one end and half at the other, all players with a ball.

The aim is to dribble the ball, stop it and leave it in the middle square and sprint to the other end to tag your teammate who can then do the same.

First team to stop all their balls in the square and get to the opposite end wins.

Note: If you have lots of balls, use them all! They can keep going until all the balls are gone and then count up which team got the most.

☐ COACHES NOTES:

- Make sure players are keeping close control while dribbling. They should be able to stop it in the square. As they approach the square encourage them to keep extra close control so they can stop it.

- Encourage the players to use the front outside part of their feet when dribbling at speed. This keeps the ball in front of them, they can look around and they can dribble faster.

☑ CHANGE IT:

#1 - Relay race: remove the middle square and have the children dribble the ball to their teammate at the other end.

#2 - Slight variation: All players start at one end (instead of at opposite ends). They dribble and leave their ball in the middle square and sprint to the opposite end then the next player goes. Once all players are at the opposite end and sit down they win the round. High fives all round!

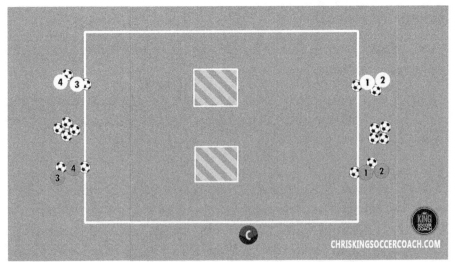

Teammates line up opposite each other, each with a ball.

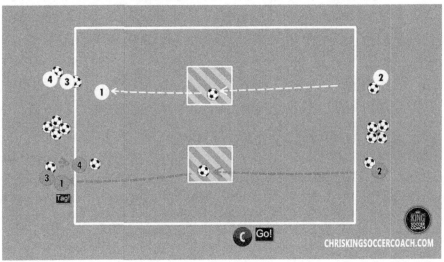

When the coach says "Go!" players dribble and stop their ball in the square and sprint to the other end. Here the Dark team is slightly ahead (Dark #1 has made it to the other end and tagged #4).

GAME #16
"MARBLES"

⬜ FOCUS OF SESSION:
Passing accuracy.

⬜ SET UP:
- **2 to 20 players**

⬜ THE DRILL:
This drill is easy to play anywhere. If for some reason you aren't organised or need to talk to a parent or another coach for a couple of minutes, this is a good game to keep the kids occupied.

Players are in pairs with a ball each.

The first player passes their ball into open space. The second player tries to pass their ball so it hits the first ball.

If a player successfully passes their ball into the other player's ball they receive 1 point. First to 5 points wins. Take it in turns of who goes first.

Note: *You can play in groups of 3 with players able to pass into either of the other two balls (1 point for hitting the closest ball or 2 points for the furthest ball).*

⬜ COACHES NOTES:
- Make sure that players look at their target but then look down at their ball as they make their pass. Players should be using the instep of their feet to pass. This has the biggest surface area. Follow through in the direction of the target.

☑ CHANGE IT:
#1 - Players receive a bonus point if they use their other (non-prefered) foot and hit the other ball.

#2 - For young kids, start each pass with the ball stationary. But for older or more skilled players can they do a skill before the pass? For example, can they do a sole roll (roll the ball with the sole of their foot) or a turn and then pass the ball? This helps improve their ability to pass a moving ball.

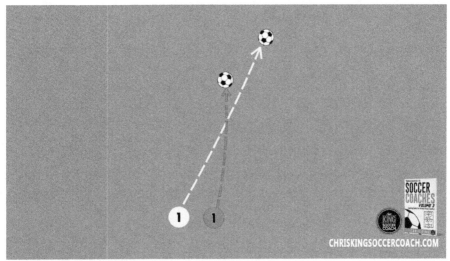

Dark has passed first. Light tried a nice firm pass to try and hit the ball but just missed. Now Dark will have a chance to hit Light's ball and receive 1 point.

GAME #17
"THE PIED PIPER"

⬚ FOCUS OF SESSION:
Dribbling, turning and changes of speed.

⬚ SET UP:
- **3 to 20 players**

⬚ THE DRILL:
This is a fun, easy drill to start training.

Give everyone a ball and then pick a leader. All the players must follow the leader and do whatever they do.

Have the leader change speed, direction and do turns, sole rolls, toe taps etc. Encourage them to do whatever they want to do. If they want to do a rolly polly, dribble backwards or dance like a chicken while they dribble, let them!

⬚ COACHES NOTES:

- Players should keep close control as they will be running into the person in front of them if they lose control.

- Change the Pied Piper (the leader) regularly and let the coach or a parent have a turn as the Pied Piper.

- Get the Pied Piper to call out what they are doing. This helps the players behind know what is happening. Plus it gives confidence to the Pied Piper and gets them used to talking to teammates which is a key part of soccer.

- Side note: "Pied" means two or more colours.

☑ CHANGE IT:
If you have too many players, make two lines.

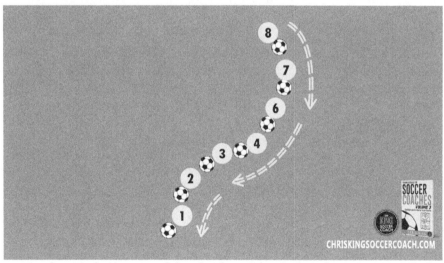

#1 is the Pied Piper and leads the rest of the players around the ground changing speed and direction, doing moves and feints that they all must copy.

GAME #18
"GATE RELAY"

⬜ FOCUS OF SESSION:

Dribbling, passing on the move, scanning the area.

☐ SET UP:

- **6 to 20 players**
- 40x30 yard rectangle

☐ THE DRILL:

Set up a large rectangle with 3 sets of gates (cones) for the players to dribble through. <u>Note</u>: Gates should be approximately 2 yards apart.

Half the team at one end and half at the other. One ball per team.

When the coach says "Go!' the first player from each team starts dribbling and must go through the gates.

Once they get 5 yards from their team mate at the other end they can pass the ball to them (this helps with the skill of passing a moving ball). Then their teammate can control the ball and dribble back through the gates the other way.

First team to finish wins.

☐ COACHES NOTES:

- Encourage the players not to kick and chase their ball. Nice and close dribbling so they have control when going through the gates.

- Look for a change of pace - once a player gets through the gate can they show a burst of pace to get to the next one?

☒ CHANGE IT:

#1 - Make the gap between the gate smaller or larger depending on the skill levels.

#2 - Have a parent (or another player) with two or three different coloured cones in their hands behind their backs. As the players are dribbling through the cones, get the parent to hold up one of the cones at random times. Players must call out the colour of the cone as they dribble. This encourages players to scan the area and get their head up while they dribble.

Note 1: You can make it so that the first player to see the cone being held up gets a bonus point.

Note 2: Alternatively, instead of cones the parent can hold up a certain amount of fingers for the player to see.

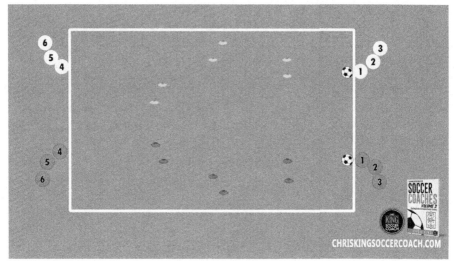

Half of each team starts at opposite ends. When the coach says "Go!" the first player from each team dribbles through the 3 sets of gates and passes the ball to their teammate at the other end.

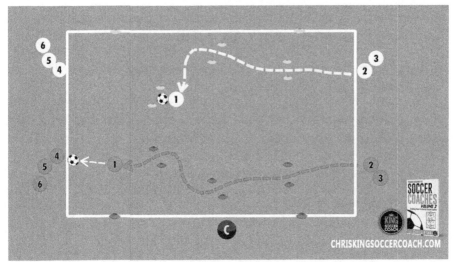

Dark #3 gets 5 yards from the end so passes to their teammate who goes back the other way. First team to finish wins.

GAME #19
"PARENTS v KIDS"

⬜ **FOCUS OF SESSION:**

Getting the parents involved.

⬜ **SET UP:**

- **4 players plus parents!**
- 40x30 yard rectangle
- 2 goals

⬜ **THE DRILL:**

Every fortnight or once a month, have a Kids v Parents game at the end (or start) of training. It gives the chance for the parents to bond and it gives the kids a chance to show them what they've been learning.

Make sure to have a quiet word with the parents so they know that the kids should end up winning ⬜.

If needed, the coach can play on the kids team to help encourage and organise them.

◻ COACHES NOTES:

- Have the maximum amount of fun! Take the mickey out of the parents. There should be lots of high fives and smiles.

☑ CHANGE IT:

Mix the teams so there are parents and kids on both teams.

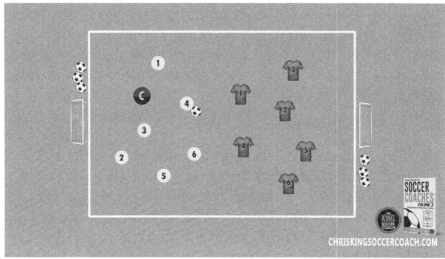

The Kids team (Light) which includes the coach versus the Parents team. Have fun!

GAME #20
"EASTER EGG HUNT"

◻ FOCUS OF SESSION:

Dribbling, shooting and maximum amounts of fun!

◻ SET UP:

- **4 to 20 players**
- 30x30 yard square
- 1 mini goal

◻ THE DRILL:

Set up a 30x30 yard square with a mini goal (the basket) at one end.

Grab as many balls as you have and get the kids to spread the balls randomly inside the square (the balls are the Easter eggs).

Kids line up behind the far line, opposite the mini goal.

The aim of the game is to get all the Easter eggs in the basket (goal) as quickly as possible! Players are all on the same team and can't tackle each other. Once they score they should be looking around to see if there are any other eggs they can put in the basket.

Here's an extra fun bit…

The coach has a Golden Egg! (a different coloured ball if possible). Once all the eggs have been put in the basket (i.e. the balls have been kicked into the goal), all the players go and hunt the coach who is dribbling the Golden Egg around the square. Whoever gets the Golden Egg off the coach and scores a goal can get the coach to do a small punishment (ie moo like a cow, roar like a lion).

 COACHES NOTES:
- Just let them go nuts. Blow the whistle and watch the chaos begin. As long as they're all laughing, yelling and scoring goals this drill has been a success.

- If possible, time them and see how long it takes to get all the balls in the goal, including the Golden Egg. Then set it up again and see if they can beat their time.

☑ CHANGE IT:
Pair players up and they can work together. They must make at least two passes before they can score.

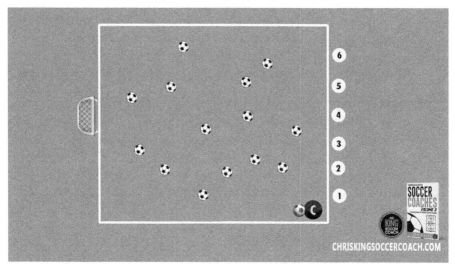

Balls are spread randomly around the square. The players must put all the eggs in the basket (kick the balls into the goal!) and then must get the last ball (The Golden Egg) off the coach.

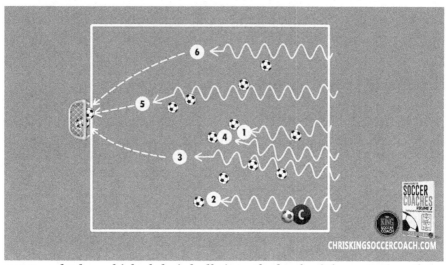

#6,5 and 3 have kicked their balls into the back of the net! The others will do the same. As soon as all the balls are in the net, the players can chase the coach around and try to get the Golden Egg (the last ball) and kick it into the goal.

Thank you for purchasing my book, I hope you got some valuable information from it. And try to keep in mind…

Every coach's main goal should be to help the kids have fun while developing their skills.

If you've enjoyed this book, please log onto Amazon and give the book a rating to help others find my book.

I also have a Facebook page and website that I post new drills and information on regularly.

www.chriskingsoccercoach.com
facebook.com/chriskingsoccercoach

Thanks again and all the best with your coaching!
Chris King

And if you need any other coaching books have a look below. I have full coaching sessions for senior players down to coaching kids soccer for parents or volunteers. All are available on Amazon or my website.

Here are some other resources that you may find useful. Most of them are free so please take full advantage to use them to improve your coaching knowledge.

WEBSITE: Head over to www.chriskingsoccercoach.com to sign up for a free eBook of soccer drills, listen to my podcast and view my other books.

AMAZON: View my other soccer coaching books on his Amazon Author Page:
USA www.amazon.com/author/chriskingsoccercoach
UK https://amzn.to/3S8As58

or just Google "Chris King Amazon books".

SCAN THE ABOVE CODE IF YOU'RE IN THE USA

SCAN THE ABOVE CODE IF YOU'RE IN THE UK

UDEMY COURSE: If you are a beginner coach I have a great online video course. It includes lots of information, games and tips for childrens soccer coaches. https://bit.ly/kidscoachingcourse

PODCAST: For coaching advice and soccer games listen to *"Coaching Kids Soccer by Chris King"* the podcast. Available on Apple, Spotify and Podbean. Also available on my website.

FACEBOOK: Join my Facebook page for free drills, updates on releases plus more. www.facebook.com/chriskingsoccercoach.

EMAIL: Please feel free to email me at chriskingsoccer@gmail.com with any feedback and what you enjoyed about the book or improvements. Or if you're a soccer coach and would like to work together to release a book just get in touch.

LEAVE A BOOK REVIEW: When you're done reading, would you please leave an honest book review on Amazon? Reviews are the BEST way to help others, and I check them looking for helpful feedback.

Amazon USA: www.am

Amazon UK: www.amazon.co.uk/

Other soccer coaching books by Chris King

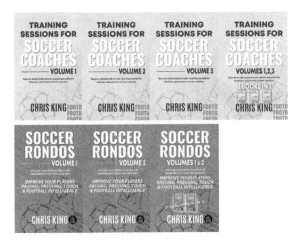

Scan the QR code below to check them out!

Author book page for those in the USA

Author book page for those in the UK